Sound Recordings

PETER COPELAND

The
British
Library

To Judy

FRONT COVER
Selection of records and sleeves, showing the prominence given to record company and shop names before the sleeves became vehicles for promoting the artists.

INSIDE FRONT COVER
Aeolian Vecalion advertisement, post-1920.

TITLE PAGE
Specially posed picture of sound effects records played for *A Streetcar Named Desire*, Aldwych Theatre, 1949.

THIS SPREAD
Examples of today's pop press — informing, entertaining, and selling records.

INSIDE BACK COVER
'Playing at BBC'.

BACK COVER
One of a series of evocative illustrations in a catalogue promoting the Edison Amberola Phonograph (see also page 73).

© 1991 The British Library Board

First published by
The British Library
Great Russell Street
London WC1B 3DG

British Library Cataloguing in Publication Data
A cataloguing record for this book is available from The British Library

ISBN 0-7123-0225-5

Designed by Roger Davies
Set on Ventura at
The Green Street Press
Colour origination by York House Graphics, Hanwell
Printed in England by Jolly & Barber Ltd, Rugby

Acknowledgements

I should like to thank the following people, all of whom have looked at parts of the manuscript and offered valuable suggestions: Crispin Jewitt, Eliot Levin, Andy Linehan, Lloyd Stickells, Adrian Tuddenham, Liz Wells, and Roger Wilmut. Much of Chapter 5 ('Fakes and Forgeries') originally appeared in *The Historic Record* magazine, and I am grateful to its Editor, Jack Wrigley, for permission to reuse the material. Thanks are also due to for Bernard Roughton for Fig. 42, and to Alistair Bamford and David Way for their patient editorial advice.

Contents

Orphée, descendant aux Enfers, dédaigne sa lyre et lui préfère le **Lioretgraph**.

— Où donc avez-vous caché l'orchestre?..
On l'entend et on ne le voit pas.
— C'est le Lioretgraph : ses rouleaux sont
inépuisables et on n'a pas besoin d'offrir des
rafraîchissements aux musiciens.

Les jours où les ministres sont absents, le
Président répond aux interpellations avec le
plus puissant des phonographes, le nouveau
Lioretgraph.

Sceaux. — Imprimerie E. Charaire.

Introduction

This book commemorates our legacy of sound recordings. The oldest datable sound recording still in existence is just over one hundred years old, so our legacy covers a much smaller span of time than books, music, or paintings. Yet in the late 20th century sound recording is still developing in a way that older media are not. I suspect that in another hundred years' time people will look back and wonder at our apparent inability to regard sound recordings as permanent media, like books, music, or paintings. Only now are we beginning to collect our legacy together, to study it, classify it, and record the circumstances in which it was born.

The purpose of the British Library's National Sound Archive is to collect sound recordings of all types. These include: commercial records; broadcasts recorded off-air; private recordings donated over the years; oral history interviews; tapes of some of Britain's leading theatre companies; railway, wildlife, and ethnic sounds collected by experts in their fields; and so on. The National Sound Archive doesn't claim to be the natural home for gramophones or other equipment, but it does have a small historical collection, because to understand the recordings, some knowledge of how they were meant to be played is desirable. This book concentrates on the recordings — the 'software' rather than the 'hardware'.

It may seem rather perverse to use the medium of the book to talk about sound recordings. But there's a need for both media — the stories lurking behind sound recordings are often quite impossible to tell in any other way. I hope this collection of information and anecdotes, which form an integral part of the story of sound recording itself, will inspire readers to visit the National Sound Archive and listen to some treasures for themselves.

LEFT
Advertisement for Lioret
Phonographs (see also page
61).

RIGHT
Listeners at the National
Sound Archive.

1 The original Tinfoil
Phonograph. Built by
Kruesi for Thomas Edison
in 1877, this machine was
on display in the Science
Museum in London until
its return to America in the
1920s.

Milestones in recording techniques

THE EMPIRICAL ERA

2 Tinfoil Record. A genuine tinfoil recording from the late 19th century. This was folded and stored in a paper envelope for nearly a hundred years, and the creases make it very unlikely we shall ever be able to play it on an original machine. Apart from anything else, it has a tendency to split, both along the creases and along the recorded undulations. Our only hope is to capture the undulations by illuminating them in a special way and then photographing them. It might then be possible to piece the photographs together and 'play' them with a photo-electric cell.

The extraordinary thing about Thomas Edison's 1877 invention for recording and playing back sound was its apparent simplicity. There is no reason why it couldn't have been invented at almost any time in the previous century — it used no new scientific knowledge, no new materials, and no new technology. The traditional story is that Edison sketched out the idea to his mechanic John Kruesi, who built it and bet a box of cigars it would not work. It is reported that Edison set it recording and spoke 'Mary had a little lamb' into it. He rewound the handle and set the machine playing. A distorted but recognizable reproduction of the nursery rhyme was heard. 'I was never so taken aback in my life', Edison later recalled. 'I was always afraid of things which worked the first time.'

But in the beginning the main aim was to achieve and maintain any intelligibility at all. Edison's first machine was the 'tinfoil phonograph' (1), in which sound waves at the mouthpiece vibrated a diaphragm, and created undulations in a stretched layer of tinfoil wrapped round a cylindrical drum. As the cylinder rotated, it was carried slowly from right to left under the mouthpiece by a screw mechanism, so consecutive lines of undulations were left in the tinfoil. Two things made intelligibility difficult. First, there was no amplification, either while the recording was taking place, or during its reproduction. All the power came from the speaker's lungs; he addressed the mouthpiece at a distance of about one inch, and projected his message at the top of his voice. Second, there was considerable background noise imposed by the tinfoil: in practice, by the way it was held in place, and its habit of crinkling from time to time. Thus the early engineers were constrained by the lack of 'signal to noise ratio' and 'sensitivity' to confine themselves to loud subject matter which could take place about one inch from the mouthpiece.

Not many genuine tinfoil records have survived from the 1870s (**2**). The main difficulty was that the tinfoil had to be wrapped round the drum each time it was loaded, and it was almost impossible to replace accurately. In the year 1887 Chichester Bell and Charles Sumner Tainter patented their improved machine, which they called 'The Graphophone' to distinguish it from Edison's 'phonograph' (**3**). The new machine recorded on cardboard cylinders covered with a coating of 'ozokerite', a wax-like material. The new principle was that a cutting tool engraved a groove in the ozokerite, which (when things were working well) cut cleanly and gave a much lower background noise. The cutting tool had a flat front face, like a chisel, and its action meant there was less impedance to the moving diaphragm, so the undulations could be greater. And, as the cardboard cylinder could be removed and replaced without crinkles, the recording retained its clarity. Even so, the Graphophone mouthpiece was not much more sensitive than that of the tinfoil phonograph. This account of a demonstration makes the point nicely: 'A cornet and piano duet was

performed in (*sic*) the instrument. Upon the record being reper-
formed, it was at least possible to tell when the pianoforte stopped
playing.'

Edison replied with an 'Improved Phonograph' (4), using solid wax
cylinders which could be shaved and reused. He originally intended
phonographs to be dictation machines in offices (5-6), so shaving and
reusing cylinders was a decided advantage. Thus, Edison-type
cylinders, two and a quarter inches in diameter, became the standard
format. But Bell and Tainter's basic principle, of *cutting* (as opposed
to indenting) to get a lower background noise, was the first milestone
in recording technology.

The next milestone was the idea of mass-producing copies of
recordings. This involved making a 'negative' version of the recording, with ridges instead of grooves, so the copies could be formed from
that. The disc records invented by Berliner were the first to possess
this advantage, since they could be stamped out almost like printing.
They also permitted a much simpler reproducing machine, since the
groove itself propelled the soundbox, no additional screw mechanism
being necessary (7). At first, the playing time for both discs and
cylinders was the same — about two minutes - but the fact that discs
could be made in different sizes, all of which could be played on the
same machine, was another advantage. In 1901 it was found that a
ten-inch disc (playing for three minutes) was better for most types of
music, even popular songs, and the popular 'single' was born.
Although cylinder manufacturers countered effectively for some
decades, first with moulding techniques and later with finer grooves,
the overwhelming simplicity of being able to press thousands of copies
of disc records and play them on a simple machine eventually told in
the disc's favour. Certainly it became economic to pay recording
artists large fees; and without mass-production, few recordings of top

7 A Berliner 'Gramophone'. An example of the machine as marketed between 1889 and 1893.

8 Studio recording. Jacques Urlus, tenor, making a recording at the Edison studio in 1916. By this date the recording machinery was kept behind curtains or screens. This was ostensibly to hide 'trade secrets', although in practice there was little new development taking place.

8a Sir Henry Wood conducting the New Queen's Hall Orchestra in one of Liszt's Hungarian Rhapsodies at Columbia's London recording studio. The date is about 1919, although the record wasn't released until 1921.

artists would survive in playable form today.

The sensitivity of Edison's original type of mouthpiece was not greatly improved. At first, people were connected to recording machines by speaking-tubes like elephants' trunks. The speaking-tube eventually evolved into a narrow horn, serving the same function - not allowing any sound to escape (8). By the mid-1900s the sensitivity of the original design had reached its maximum. A conical horn with an opening perhaps one foot in diameter faced into the recording room. This could pick up perhaps two or three selected artists chosen for their recording prowess, the others in the recording room being relegated to 'accompaniment'. Even the foreground artists had to be specially selected, because not everyone was willing or able to adapt his technique. It was necessary to project the vowel-sounds forcefully but *evenly*, and to exaggerate the consonants. 'R's were always rolled, for example, and 'S's were not only delivered forcefully but with a quality more like the 'Sh' sound, to which the diaphragm responded better. It is interesting that nearly all music-hall artists adapted

9 Classical piano recording. An attempt to capture as much sound from a piano as possible. With modern knowledge, we now know that this design of horn would have reflected more sound than it captured!

successfully; evidently, years of projecting the voice over the orchestra and up towards the upper circle without the help of loudspeakers was good training.

For years, the technique was kinder to the voice than to most musical instruments. Only instruments with rather a metallic sound recorded well: the solo banjo, the brass band, and percussion instruments such as bells and xylophones. Both the extreme bass and the extreme treble were lost, so most of the standard drum-kit (which normally provides the rhythm above and below the pitch of the instruments carrying the melody) was banned from the studio. This gives us an unbalanced picture of dance band and jazz arrangements today. Dance bands recording acoustically had to arrange their tunes to place strong rhythm into the banjo and piano parts, with only the occasional punctuation from cymbal or woodblock to represent the percussion section. It is even possible that acoustic recording techniques dictated the popularity of the fox-trot, which to modern ears is a very four-square and unsophisticated rhythm. Yet some of the very earliest jazz bands, recorded before companies pretended to 'understand' the new music, do have a complete drum-kit in the background. Played on old machines, the drum-kit is not at all clear; it sounds like a dull roar behind the front line. But with modern electronic compensation, one finds the drum-kit is reasonably well captured. It was therefore the playback process that caused the banning of the drum-kit. We must remember 'he who pays the piper calls the tune', and record producers influenced what we hear today. Popular music's 'standard hit' three minutes long remained the norm for nearly a century, and was only liberated by the 'twelve-inch single'.

Classical music fared even less well. The following list of aesthetic compromises is by no means complete, but it illustrates how early recording artists had to adapt. Pianos always caused difficulties, because the sounds came from a sounding-board with a large area (**9**). So the piano was nearly always an upright, which was also easier to get close to the horn. The back was taken off so there would be nothing between the sounding-board and the horn, and the pianist was instructed to play 'double forte' throughout (**10**). Sometimes the piano's hammers were re-covered with something harder than felt, because of the diaphragm's insensitivity to transient sounds. There was little improvement in the diaphragm's sensitivity after about 1906, but better manufacturing techniques (resulting in less surface

10 State-of-the-art piano recording. A piano accompaniment being captured in a London recording studio of 1904.

noise) and better gramophones (with greater efficiency) meant that by 1920 classical pianists could be recorded playing relatively unmodified grand pianos.

Orchestras were even more problematic (11). String instruments always raised difficulties, because they had less power than the wind section, and their operators needed more 'elbow-room'. The Stroh Violin was commonly employed; this was a violin fitted with a soundbox and horn so the upper harmonics of violin tone could be directed at the recording machine. Players were encouraged to exaggerate the portamento and vibrato features of their instruments to help distinguish them from the wind sections (11). French horn players sat with their backs to the machine so their instruments blasted straight at it; they viewed the conductor in a mirror. As bass notes were reproduced very weakly, the bass line was often attributed to the tuba, which had more higher-frequency harmonics; these could be recognized on playback as constituting a 'bass line'. Bass could also be reinforced by careful choice of recording horn, which added low-pitched resonances of its own. Stage management was needed during a 'take' to give soloists uninterrupted access. Vocalists had to bob down out of the way during instrumental breaks, and those unfamiliar with recording technique had to be man-handled by the recording director to bring them close to the horn on low notes and push them further away on high notes. These compromises, resulting in records which were considered musically acceptable in those days, mean ethical decisions when we come to play them back today; should we even *try* to restore the original 'fidelity'?

The cure to all these difficulties was obvious — amplification. And between the years 1905 and 1925 many inventors worked on the problem. A mechanical amplifier had been envisaged by Edison in 1877, and an electronic amplifier by Lee de Forest in 1914; but there proved to be more to solving the problem than that. It was necessary to design a complete system, comprising a high-quality microphone, accurately matched to a high-quality electronic amplifier, which was accurately matched to a high-quality electromagnetic cutter. Ignoring any one parameter would give disappointing results, and this was why at least four teams of British inventors failed. Each produced the three components, but did not get a successful overall result.

One, however, qualified for the distinction of making the first electrical recording to be sold to the public. This was recorded by the Hon. Lionel Guest and Captain H. O. Merriman at the Burial Service of the Unknown Warrior at Westminster Abbey on 11 November 1920. Only two hymns seem to have been recorded, presumably because the anonymity of the subject-matter meant no copyright complications. The record was pressed (in at least two runs of 500 copies each) by the Columbia company for the Abbey Restoration Fund (12). Surviving copies are very faint, distinctly telephonic in

12 Label of 'Abide with me' recorded at the Westminster Abbey Burial Service of the Unknown Soldier.

13 *The Illustrated London News* published this illustration of the technology used to produce the Westminster Abbey recording.

quality, and start with an appalling wow because the cutter was engaged before the wax was up to speed; but an account in the *Illustrated London News* (**13**) shows the disposition of the microphones and the apparatus, which amount to a full recording system in the modern sense. With the benefit of hindsight, we can see that the disappointing results were largely caused by the use of telephone mouthpieces (in the absence of better microphones), and a cutter whose moving parts had too much inertia. It is a clear example of the point that a successful electrical recording system had to be planned with consistent quality and matching equipment from first to last. Scientific methods would have to be adopted.

DRAWN BY OUR SPECIAL ARTIST, W. B. ROBINSON, FROM MATERIAL SUPPLIED BY MAJOR THE HON. LIONEL GUEST AND CAPTAIN H. O. MERRIMAN.

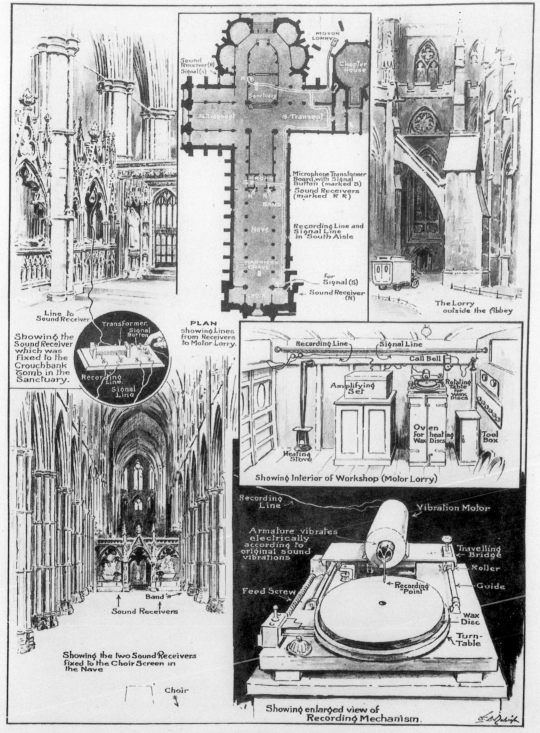

Line to
Sound Receiver

Showing the
Sound Receiver
which was
Fixed to the
Crouchbank
Comb in the
Sanctuary.

Transformer,
Signal Button

Recording
Line

Signal
Line

PLAN
showing Lines
from Receivers
to Motor Lorry.

MOTOR
LORRY

Sound Receiver (R)
Signal (s)

Chapter
House

Sanctuary

N. Transept

S. Transept

Microphone Transformer
Board, with Signal
Button (marked S)
Sound Receivers
(marked R R)

Recording Line and
Signal Line
in South Aisle

Nave

WARRIORS
GRAVE

for
Signal (S)

Sound Receiver
(R)

CHOIR

The Lorry
outside the Abbey

Recording Line   Signal Line

Call Bell

Amplifying
Set

Rotating
Table
for
Wax Discs

Oven
for heating
Wax Discs

Tool
Box

Healing
Stove

Showing Interior of Workshop (Motor Lorry)

Band
Sound Receivers

Showing the two Sound Receivers
fixed to the Choir Screen in
the Nave

Choir

Recording
Line

Vibration Motor

Armature vibrates
electrically
according to
original sound
vibrations

Travelling
Bridge

Roller

Guide

Feed Screw

Recording
"Point"

Wax
Disc

Turn-
Table

Showing enlarged view of
Recording Mechanism.

HOW MUSIC AT THE ABBEY BURIAL OF THE UNKNOWN WARRIOR WAS RECORDED IN A LORRY OUTSIDE

Milestones in recording techniques

THE SCIENTIFIC ERA

Experiments in electrical recording continued, but the most significant research took place at the Western Electric laboratories in New York. Two researchers, Joseph P. Maxfield and Henry C. Harrison, planned a system which could record sounds between frequencies of 100 Hertz and 4500 Hertz, and each piece of apparatus was designed to meet this specification. They also used the principle known to electrical engineers as 'matched impedance'. This describes how two pieces of electrical equipment can be connected so there is no waste of power at the connection. But Maxfield and Harrison took the principle further by applying it to acoustic and mechanical parts, so that there would be little waste of power from 'mismatching' at any point along the sound's journey. Their system also included a sophisticated design for an acoustic reproducer to play the new records.

A microphone was installed at the nearby Capitol Theater to provide high-fidelity subject matter, and the resulting waxes were sent to the Pathé factory in Brooklyn to be made into ordinary pressings. Frank Capps of Pathé made some additional unauthorized pressings and sent them to Louis Sterling of Columbia in London. They arrived on Christmas Eve 1924, proving that high-quality electrical test recordings existed at the end of 1924, although it is not known that any of these survive today. After some delay, Western Electric equipment was set up at Victor's studios in Camden, New Jersey. A few years ago, historians thought that Victor 19626 was the first commercially published electrical recording; but in 1980 Robert W. Baumbach revealed in his book *Look For The Dog* that some earlier test recordings were eventually issued, which were not publicized because Victor had not signed the contract with Western Electric at the time. The earliest he cites is the first side of 'A Miniature Concert', recorded on 26 February 1925 and issued on Victor 35753 (and in Britain on Zonophone A302). However, I recently discovered a copy of English Columbia 3748 which bore the symbol of the Western Electric system punched into the label-surround. It was a record of Art Gillham, the Whispering Pianist, singing 'I Had Someone Else Before I Had You'. Brian Rust's book *The Complete Entertainment Discography* states that it was recorded in New York on 25 February 1925, so this American Columbia electrical recording seems to be earlier, by one day.

The Benefits of Amplification

On 31 March 1925 American Columbia used their new equipment to record a most impressive demonstration disc — the Associated Glee Clubs of America at the Metropolitan Opera House. The microphone not only captured 850 voices in perfect balance, something impossible with acoustic techniques, but it also caught the bass strings of the grand piano accurately, and the acoustic environment of the Opera

House around the performance.

The Western Electric system was thoroughly thought out, with a performance exceeding acoustic cutters by two-and-a-half octaves and almost unlimited amplification. The effects upon the actual records overshadowed some equally great revolutions behind the scenes, which tend to be forgotten.

First among these was that the engineers could listen to what they were doing upon a loudspeaker in a nearby room. Thus it was possible for engineers to place their microphone to give a ratio of direct and reflected sound from the walls of the studio in order to achieve a pleasing artistic reproduction. Also, recording engineers could 'tame' performances of wide dynamic range, so that loud passages would not overload the cutter (or give repeating grooves in the master-wax), and soft passages would not get lost behind the surface noise. Many experiments were done to decide who should have responsibility for controlling the sound; but eventually it all came down to the engineers, assisted by meters and (most important of all) a keen musical sense.

'Natural' and 'Unnatural' Recordings

From this period onwards, sound recordings can be divided into two types. First, we have those recordings which are 'natural', in the sense that they aim to reproduce the original subject-matter. Secondly, we have 'unnatural' recordings, in which original sounds (or in some cases electrical waveforms which have never even had a separate acoustic existence) are subject to processes which make them into something new. The connotations of the words 'natural' and 'unnatural' should not be overemphasised; indeed, the purpose of 'unnatural' techniques is often to simulate and reproduce natural sounds. For example, sound recording for films and television is done with a monstrous array of equipment and techniques. One might reasonably wonder how or why these recording processes came to be introduced if 'naturalness' were the aim. But the problems of keeping microphones out of the picture, of different versions for foreign countries, and of editing the pictures independently of sound, mean such processes have become inevitable. It is greatly to the credit of the profession that, as viewers, we are not aware of the many techniques which have been used to produce a 'natural' effect.

The technical processing of sound therefore has two functions. It allows the engineers to achieve something which would not be possible otherwise and which seems natural to the audience. On the other hand it also allows new artistic effects to be employed if desired. A hoary example of both at once is the filming of a dialogue scene during a howling gale, while a full symphony orchestra plays in the background.

Today there are so many 'unnatural' recordings being made,

14 A divided orchestra. Leopold Stokowski conducts an orchestra which has been divided into individually-miked sections for increased clarity. But there is a limit to how much can be done on these lines, because the sections have to be able to hear each other to maintain precise rhythm.

including recordings for specific art-forms such as pop music, that the 'natural' type of sound recording is now in decline. Many of the most important milestones are in post-production techniques, rather than inherent improvements in the 'naturalness' of pure sound recording. Any account of these milestones has to bear both applications in mind.

It did not take long for engineers to realise they could use more than one microphone, and 'balance' the music internally. Indeed, the *Illustrated London News* shows that Guest & Merriman's experiment had included several microphones and a selector system, but the surviving disc shows no sign of active 'mixing'. Before long, engineers were performing sound-mixing functions hitherto the responsibility of the conductor or musical director. One of the earliest collaborators was the conductor Leopold Stokowski, who happily agreed to experiments to divide the Philadelphia Orchestra into individually miked sections for increased clarity, presumably in search of something more like the clarity he perceived from the conductor's rostrum (14). One may argue that this was the beginning of 'unnatural' recording techniques.

Early Film Sound

The principal impetus behind 'unnatural' techniques was in fact the talking picture, which became a reality in about 1928. Although pure sound recording had started in America, the moving picture was probably America's greatest contribution to world culture. The early days of talkies in Hollywood must have been one of the steepest learning-curves anyone anywhere has faced. Unfortunately, the exact history of the techniques used has never been recorded. People were presumably far too busy at the time, and the principal workers have now died. But in three short years the following essential features of creative sound were worked out for the first time: cut-and-splice sound editing; dubbing mute shots (i.e. providing library sounds for completely silent bits of film); quiet cameras; 'talkback' and other intercom systems; 'boom' microphones (so the mike could be placed over the actor's head and moved as necessary); equalization; track-bouncing; replacement of dialogue (including alternative languages); filtering (for removing traffic noise, wind noise, or for simulating telephone conversations); busbars for routing controlled amounts of foldback or reverberation; three-track recording (music, effects, and dialogue, any of which could be changed as necessary); automatic volume limiters; and synchronous playback (for dance or mimed shots). By 1931 all these techniques were routine, and it is a

15 *Blackmail.* A shot taken on the set of Britain's first sound film in 1929. Note that it has been necessary to enclose the camera behind a glass screen to cut down its noise. The director (wearing headphones) is Alfred Hitchcock. The actress, Anny Ondra, had a pronounced Czech accent, so her speech was not recorded synchronously.

very great pity that the people who developed them cannot now be identified.

Britain was not far behind. The first talkie made in Britain, Alfred Hitchcock's *Blackmail* (1929), shows several creative uses of 'unnatural' technique. One was forced upon the director because the film was originally planned to be 'silent'. The heroine was played by the Czech actress Anny Ondra (**15** and **15a**). She spoke almost no English, and her voice was dubbed synchronously by Joan Barry. The famous sequence where the heroine cannot stop thinking about the blood-stained knife, and keeps overhearing the word 'knife' in her father's newsagent's shop, is also an unparalleled use of sound technique .

Multi-Tracking

While the film industry was leading with innovative techniques, there were nevertheless some developments conducted by the sound industry on its own. First of these was 'multi-tracking', by which one musician appears to give the performances of two or more. This involves recording one line of music (the 'backing' or 'rhythm' track), which is then played back to the musician while a second line is added. The earliest example I've come across involves a banjo player named Patti, who recorded two numbers like this in Brunswick's New York studio in June 1932. A similar technique was used by Victor the following August to provide a new orchestra behind some of Caruso's acoustic recordings, with their distant tinny accompaniments. In England, the complete technique was applied to serious music; in September 1935 Elisabeth Schumann recorded both parts of the Evening Prayer from Humperdinck's *Hansel und Gretel*. As I've described it above, the process differs from modern multi-track technique, because the 'backing track' went through a number of generations, while modern multi-track tape recorders keep each layer separate; so the technique wasn't used as fully as it might have been, because the quality dropped each time. Even professional tape-recorders after the war could not keep the quality high enough for more than two or three generations. The guitarist Les Paul, together with his vocalist wife Mary Ford, recorded many hit tunes for Capitol from the end of 1948 onwards, but history is silent about the hours of trial-and-error (mainly error) this must have involved. The craze hit England in 1951, when musicians such as Larry Adler, Steve Race and Humphrey Lyttelton (the latter emulating a traditional jazz band in his *One Man Went To Blow*) attempted to make a whole which was greater than the sum of the parts. Nowadays the technique is normal in pop music (**16**).

The Idea of Stereo

Another innovation by the sound studios was stereophonic recording. The purpose was not so much to reproduce the direction of artists as

15a 'You ought to have been more careful. Might have cut somebody with that.' Charles Paton's line to Anny Ondra, as she drops the bread-knife during breakfast after the murder. A scene from *Blackmail* (1929)

16 Multi-tracked records. All these records feature artists playing two or more parts. The LP at the back is the supreme example of this, Mike Oldfield's *Tubular Bells*, in which he played all the parts of 45 minutes of music composed by himself. It was issued in 1973.

17 The first stereo microphone. Invented by Alan Blumlein in 1931, this comprises two ribbon microphone elements with a common magnet system. The two ribbons are most sensitive to sounds arriving from forty-five degrees on either side of the central axis.

to circumvent the unnatural effect of 'music coming out of a hole'. Experiments in Paris involving transmission by telephone lines date back to 1881, but it needed the technology of the 1930s to record two channels with adequate fidelity, synchronization and separation. Once again, Stokowski and the Philadelphia Orchestra were in the forefront. Two excerpts from Scriabin's *Poem of Fire* were recorded on stereo discs on 12 March 1932. These were followed on later dates by other experimental recordings. As far as we know, they all used two or three microphones spaced some yards apart along the front of the orchestra, a technique favoured by American engineers to this day.

Meanwhile, Alan Blumlein of EMI in Britain was working in ignorance of developments in America; his concept was to record two optical channels on cine film. But when delivery of the required 'four-ribbon light valve' was delayed, he turned to disc recording so he could have permanent records of his experiments. This work was in some ways inferior to that done in America, where engineers had developed a disc-cutter with better frequency-range and lower distortion, and their pressings had lower surface-noise as well. But Blumlein invented a completely different microphone technique, the 'coincident' technique (**17**), and showed how compatible mono recordings and '45/45' stereo discs (eventually adopted as the world standard in 1958) could be obtained with the technique. And, when the light-valve was finally delivered in 1934, he made some stereo variable-area optical soundtracks almost identical to those adopted by the film industry in the late 1970s.

Long-Playing Records

The 1930s were also a time for experimental long-playing records. But what one means by 'the first LP' depends very much on your definition of LP; long-playing records of various types date back to the 1900s, as we shall see later. The stimulus in the 1930s was, again, the cinema; for patent reasons, some studios preferred to distribute their films with separate disc soundtracks, rather than have the sound printed optically on the film itself. To match a 1000ft reel of film which ran for a little over eleven minutes, a 78rpm turntable had to be slowed to 33 1/3rpm (**18**). This speed was then adopted for Victor's first long-playing records of 1931-34. Although imperfect marketing has been cited by historians as the reason for Victor's failure, in fact there may have been a simple operational reason. It was difficult enough to cut a perfect master 78rpm disc with a duration of only five minutes. To cut a perfect long-playing side without stopping imposed intolerable demands on everyone. Stokowski and the Philadelphia Orchestra (again!) recorded Beethoven's *Fifth Symphony* in this manner; but Victor's other LPs had to be patched-up dubbings from standard records, and they had a distinctly second-hand quality. The only great successes Victor had were spoken records, including

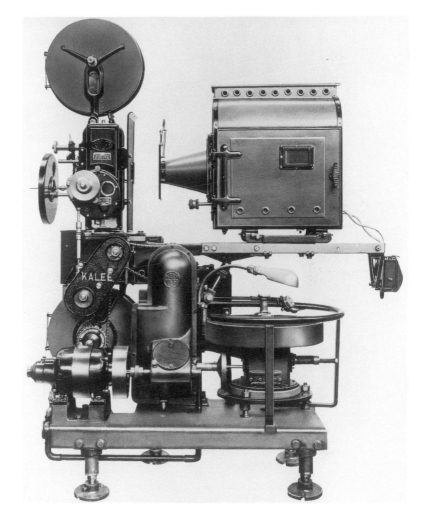

18 Early film projector. This machine was used in cinemas in the late 1920s. It reproduced the soundtrack from a disc record underneath the lamp housing. Both the projector and the turntable were powered by the same motor to ensure they ran at the same speed. Projectionists had to be very careful to orientate the disc and to put the pickup in the right groove for the sound to be in synchronism.

training courses for advertising and sales people, and innumerable Health Talks by a Dr Copeland. This subject-matter permitted long runs which were no more difficult to create than broadcasts. The 33 1/3 rpm speed was taken up by radio stations, and used for their internal purposes until the 1950s. Meanwhile, commercial long-playing records of music had to await a high-quality mastering format which could be edited — in other words, magnetic tape.

Full Frequency-Range Recording

But before tape came along, the record industry came up with one more development - full frequency-range recording. The idea of a recording system covering the full range perceived by the human ear dates back to 1925, when Brunswick claimed their electrical recordings covered the range from 16Hz to 21000Hz (**19**). However, surviving discs show the upper limit was more like 4000Hz, inferior to Western Electric's 4500Hz. By 1934 the highest frequency which

19 Brunswick record sleeve. The Brunswick Company claimed their 'Light Ray Process' could cover the full frequency range perceived by the human ear, but this was the first of many such false claims. The A. & P. Gypsies, by the way, were among the very first stars to have a radio 'series' — a programme which was broadcast regularly from the same station at the same time of the same day of the week.

could reliably be recorded had reached 8000Hz. In 1940 the British Decca Company was asked by RAF Coastal Command if it could record frequencies up to 14000Hz, almost the limit of human hearing. This was because officers listening to sonar buoys needed this frequency response to distinguish between Allied and German submarines, and they needed a set of training-records. In 1941 Arthur Haddy, Decca's chief engineer, solved the problem, and the new cutter was put into use for commercial recording (**20**). But before airborne sound could be accurately recorded, he had to develop a microphone with comparable performance, the Decca FR1. Decca's Full Frequency-Range Recording (FFRR) system was publicized in June 1945, and the improvement was especially noticeable on massed strings. Decca's first official FFRR recording, Tchaikovsky's *Fifth Symphony*, was a good advertisement; but equally important were the effects on popular music. It is inconceivable that Edmundo Ros's maraccas, or Mantovani's string sound, could have become famous without full-range recording.

The Development of Magnetic Recording

The principles of magnetic recording had been around for a long time. The Dane Valdemar Poulsen invented his 'Telegraphone' in 1898 and

20 Decca 'ffrr' disc recorder. The world's first machine capable of recording the full frequency range of the human ear. Most of the cutter comprised a powerful electromagnet, hanging over the turntable from the ceiling because of its weight.

21 Steel-tape magnetic recorder, as used by the BBC in the 1930s.

22 An AEG magnetic recorder. This model was first exhibited at the German Radio Exhibition in August 1934. It could record upon 'normal' recording tape, comprising a coating of ferric oxide on a non-magnetic base.

patented it in 1900, but (as with commercial electrical recording) amplification was needed before it could become practicable. The principles of the electronic valve were applied to magnetic recording in the late 1920s, so the BBC used steel-tape recorders for repeating programmes for the Empire broadcasting service (21).

Despite some significant developments by BBC and Marconi engineers, the system still did not give better quality than 78rpm discs; it only succeeded because it gave longer running-time, and it had lower running-costs because the tape could be magnetically erased and reused. It was a combination of inventions that proved to hold the secret to quality. The two most important were iron-oxide coated plastic tape (first produced in Germany in 1934) (22) and ultrasonic alternating-current bias (patented by Carlson and Carpenter in the USA in 1921). The latter invention was an accidental discovery, made when a faulty recording amplifier developed ultrasonic oscillations, and the reason why it worked was very difficult to explain. So the two inventions were not combined until 1940. Shortly afterwards, listeners monitoring German broadcasts became aware that Hitler could not be broadcasting 'live' from so many places at once. Yet there was an absence of surface-noise which showed that discs could not possibly have been used. The mystery was solved when the Allies captured Radio Luxembourg in 1944, where they found a new type of magnetic tape recorder combining the two inventions already mentioned. Its performance exceeded that of contemporary discs. Within three years, American broadcasters and record companies had abandoned discs as a mastering medium. Economic conditions made this process slower in Britain, but by 1950 the new technology was coming into use at the gramophone studios, permitting the first LPs to be made.

Tape editing is, of course, another 'unnatural' process. Although I have mentioned the analagous process with optical film, as far as I can discover magnetic tape was first spliced to make a BBC radio programme. It was called 'Pieces of Tape', an anthology of broadcasts from the year 1932 which was transmitted on 13 January 1933. An extract from this programme has been preserved in the BBC Sound Archive. The steel tape had to be cut with wire-cutters, then soldered, and then it had to be 'tempered' before it could run through the

23 Tape-editing today. The editor is about to splice two pieces of tape, which he has marked with yellow pencil and cut with a razor blade. Adhesive splicing-tape is applied to the back, so the oxide surface remains uninterrupted.

machine — which it did with a loud clang! After the war, plastic-based iron-oxide tape could be cut with non-magnetic scissors (or even a razor-blade), and either welded with cement or stuck with adhesive tape (23). It then went through the machine silently. To the dismay of record-collectors, it now became possible to piece together a collection of imperfect bits to make a complete note-perfect performance. Nowadays record collectors have accepted this process, and only complain if they hear an imperfect edit, while record producers exercise their skills in an attempt to preserve the spontaneous qualities of a performance as well as the note-perfect quality.

From 1945 onwards there were steady improvements in magnetic tape. By 1970 a professional full-track mono tape recorder could just about achieve a signal-to-noise ratio of 70 decibels, while the full frequency range could just about be squeezed onto a tape cassette running at 1.875 inches per second. But tape 'hiss' remained a limiting factor, especially in stereo, and it was easy to hear the tape hiss start up on LP records. Dr Ray Dolby introduced his professional tape noise-reduction system ('Dolby A') at the British Decca studios in 1966, and the system gradually spread through the profession, adding another ten decibels to the potential dynamic range. His simpler 'Dolby B' system was adopted for tape cassettes in 1971, and was the main reason why this format became so popular as a means of disseminating commercially prerecorded material. Although even the best tape cassettes could not outperform the best LPs, they were much more rugged, and did not develop annoying clicks. By 1985 sales of tape cassettes were outnumbering disc sales, although it had taken 40 years for the advocates of magnetic recording to see this come about.

Digital Sound and the Future

In less than a century the world of sound-recording had expanded from a plaything for amateurs to a world-wide billion-dollar industry, and it looks set to stay that way. But in the meantime another form of recording was on the way — 'digital recording'. The principle horrified hi-fi buffs when it was first announced, because it chopped the sound wave up at an ultrasonic rate and described each 'slice' as a binary number. Digital techniques had initially been invented to cram more telephone conversations into a single cable, because 'crosstalk' does not affect a string of numbers. Digital techniques were also used during the US space missions because of a unique advantage — the possibility of error correction. In 1969 the BBC used digital sound for distributing its television soundtracks from London to the regions within the synchronization pulses of the television picture. This gave better sound quality and avoided the cost of audio landlines at the same time. Then in 1972 the BBC adopted digits for the technically demanding radio network, at that time being converted to stereo; and in the same year the Nippon Columbia record company started mastering its records digitally. Their '14-bit' system offered a potential signal-to-noise ratio of about 84 decibels. Because digital audio implies a great many binary numbers, an ordinary tape-recorder could not record them; so a broadcast video recorder was used instead (**24**). Other experimental systems followed. By 1982, Sony's system, using its U–Matic videocassettes for storing '16-bit' digital audio (with a potential signal-to-noise ratio of some 96 decibels), had become an industry standard.

Meanwhile, Philips in Holland had been pioneering the use of 'Laservision' videodiscs, the least unsuccessful of several types of disc for carrying video films. These were played by a beam of laser light rather than a stylus, and Philips saw that combining digital audio with laser disc technology would be a great improvement upon the Dolby Cassette and the LP. The 'Compact Digital Disc' (CD) came on the market in 1982, and has now practically replaced the LP as a distribution medium. '16-bit' audio has a signal-to-noise ratio which comfortably exceeds the full dynamic range of an orchestra, so it became possible to record orchestral music without any need to compress its dynamic range.

The main advantage of digital recording is that, in principle, it can be copied without degrading, because error-correction restores the original digits each time. Of course, this worries the record companies,

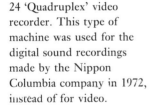

24 'Quadruplex' video recorder. This type of machine was used for the digital sound recordings made by the Nippon Columbia company in 1972, instead of for video.

because the potential for piracy is great. At the time of writing it seems that digital tape recorders sold to the public will have various anti-piracy measures built into them for this very reason. On the other hand, error- correction pleases the record producers, because compact digital discs sold in the shops sound exactly like the master-tape in the studio. And archivists like it, because if the medium carrying the recording has a limited life, it is possible to copy the sound to another medium without any degradation taking place.

In practice, all media do have a limited life. A search is now under way to find a medium with a reliably long shelf-life, because even if our present-day sound recordings last for a full century (which is doubtful), our successors will have to copy the whole collection every hundred years or so. For analog sound-recording, experience has shown that the metal masters used in the process of pressing disc copies have a very long life. But this is a very expensive way of preserving sound, only tolerable when hundreds of copies are likely to be sold to cover the costs. In addition, the business of cutting a master is a highly skilled craft, and at present it is a dying art. Archivists are therefore thinking of combining digital technology with robust media.

One major problem is that you can never prove the life of an item. The best that scientists can do is to submit specimens to an 'Arrhenius Test', based on a formula by the Swedish physicist Arrhenius, which predicts the rate at which chemical reactions will occur. In this way, it is possible to estimate how the chemical stability of a sound recording will fare with time. The Conservation Laboratory of the British Library National Sound Archive is undertaking research on these lines at the moment, and the strongest candidate is a form of computer WORM disk (Write Once, Read Many times). Such disks can be used to store other things besides sound recordings, such as text, graphics, printed music, manuscripts, and moving pictures, so the research has wide applications for collections of the whole of the British Library and beyond. Everyone hopes that a programme of copying the holdings of the National Sound Archive to a more rugged medium will start soon — and that brings us a new challenge. We must be certain we can do justice to the wonderful things past engineers have bequeathed us.

Labels

Documentation of sound recordings is almost as important as the sounds themselves. There is no point in keeping exciting sounds if you don't know what they are, or if you can't find them. So there has always been a need to attach labels to audio media, whether written descriptions on sheets of paper or in some other form.

Edison's tinfoil records, and both kinds of wax cylinder (for Phonograph and Graphophone), were only transitory media. There was no impetus to develop anything more sophisticated than a spoken announcement or a separate piece of paper packed into the box. This means that many cylinder records surviving today have highly dubious provenances, as we shall see later.

It is debatable whether it was the cylinder or the disc that was the first to have a formal 'label' physically attached. At the 1890 Convention of Local Phonograph Companies in Chicago, delegates asked for a longer cylinder with a section specifically set aside for an announcement, but this did not come about. The following year there was a visit to the Edison works at West Orange, where the delegates saw prerecorded cylinders made by an experimental moulding process. The next day Walter Miller of the Edison Company was asked whether all the musical records he sent would have the title on the end of the cylinder, as they had seen arranged at the laboratory the day before, to which he replied, 'Yes sir, they will be fixed up that way'. However, it was not to be; the Edison company preferred to market the phonograph as a dictation machine, and nearly a decade went by before cylinder moulding became a commercial reality.

In the meantime, Berliner's first disc records were made in Germany, and these definitely had 'labels' of a sort (**25, 26**). The only doubt concerns the date; it seems these early records could be from any year between 1889 and 1891, so whether Edison or Berliner was actually first to make records with a 'label' is open to debate.

The conventional paper label was never possible on a cylinder, since there was insufficient flat space. The end of the cylinder box had to suffice (**27**), and paper labels were not attached to discs until 1901 (**28**, left). It should be pointed out that they were nearly always pressed into the disc at the time of manufacture, not pasted on afterwards; so the paper and inks had to be able to withstand high temperatures. This is one reason why metallic inks, such as gold or silver, were common. In later years, paper labels served another function: they acted like gaskets, preventing molten material from getting into the mechanism for punching the centre hole.

Half a century later, when vinyl discs became the norm, there was another complication. Vinyl required greater temperatures in the press, and the molten material flowed with much less viscosity. So if ordinary paper labels curled up during the manufacturing process, they would take the vinyl with them, resulting in a warped disc. Specialist label printers appeared, selling 'grain-oriented' paper. This

25 Berliner disc 'label'. No paper label was used; instead the information was engraved into the master-disc and reproduced on every copy together with the sound. The title is the very last word scratched on the master, in this case 'Loriley', a traditional German melody.

26 Berliner disc. This was one of the first disc records to be marketed in Britain. It is five inches in diameter and single-sided, and comprises 'The Lord's Prayer'. This was a popular title in the early talking-machine industry. Everyone knew the words, so they could follow the distorted reproduction successfully.

27 Cylinder boxes. The ends of cylinder boxes carried the nearest the cylinder format ever got to labels.

28 Paper labels for discs. The left-hand record carries an example of the first type of paper label for discs, introduced in 1901. The right-hand record carries an early example of a 'red label'. They sold for twice the price of a 'black label' record.

was not only designed to withstand the heat without soaking up liquid vinyl like blotting-paper, but it was supplied with a distinctive pattern on the back to indicate the direction of the paper grain. When two labels were inserted in the press with their grains at right-angles, any tendency for the paper to distort in one direction in preference to the other was neutralized.

Returning to the beginning of the century: the idea of a coloured label to signify a quality recording came from Raphoff, a Gramophone retailer in St Petersburg, in April 1901. A year later the first 'red label' records were on the market (**28**, right). By the 1920s an elaborate hierarchy of colours indicated the position of the record within a class system; the overall range of prices varied over the years, but not the implied class structure. So far as the original Gramophone Company was concerned, dark green was at the bottom of the pecking-order, although in Britain such records carried a different trade-name, Zonophone. Prices were highest in 1922; twelve-inch records from The Gramophone Company were between four and twenty shillings each (**31**).

By 1905, all makers of prerecorded cylinders were marking the actual cylinders with titles by means of a professional lettering process, though the techniques used varied widely from company to company (**29**). The idea of filling the engravings with white greatly added to the legibility, but the conventional cylinder (just over two inches in diameter) had insufficient space for much more than the title. This didn't matter very much as cylinders soon found themselves right at the bottom of the class structure of recordings, and not many featured artists worth naming.

As disc records took a greater hold of the market, some cylinder companies turned to discs; but many of them eschewed paper labels. Pathé discs adopted the idea of filling the engraved letters with white (**30**), but Edison's 'Diamond Discs' did not (**32**). Incidentally, most disc manufacturers with double-sided discs called the two sides 'A' and 'B'. But Edison identified his two sides by 'L' and 'R', presumably for 'Left' and 'Right'; clearly they were being regarded as very short fat cylinders!

The Copyright Act of 1911 forced record manufacturers to pay royalties to music composers (or their publishers). This was enforced by a system of adhesive stamps, the value of which was calculated to provide a royalty of five per cent of the retail cost of the record (*see* **31c**). The Act permitted such stamps to be affixed to the container, rather than the record itself; this was the only practicable way with cylinders. But the Board of Trade had a great deal of latitude to vary the precise details of the arrangement, and insisted that, for discs, the records should bear the stamps, not the sleeves. As it was difficult to make stamps adhere to records without paper labels, by 1916 all disc companies were using them.

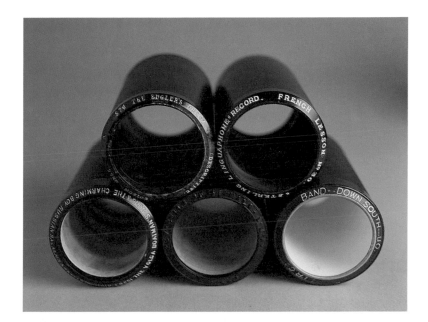

29 Ends of cylinder records, showing the lettering styles used by different manufacturers.

30 Pathé disc label.

a

b

c

d

e

f

g

h

i

j

31 (a to j) The Gramophone Company class system. All these records are twelve inches in diameter and were made by the Gramophone Company of Great Britain between 1920 and 1925. The different coloured labels represent different prices, which in turn reflected the eminence of the performer(s). Quantity as well as quality entered this calculation; the buff label (**31f**) featured two 'Red Label' artists, the pale green (**31g**) featured four, and the white (**31i**) four on one side and six on the other. But the top of the range featured the solo tenor Francesco Tamagno. He was the first artist to insist upon royalty payments, and his contract stipulated that the records should be retailed at £1.00 each. He made his recordings in 1904 and died a year later; by 1925 they had been moved to the 'Historic Catalogue'.

32 Edison 'diamond disc' label.

It was many years before the collection agencies and the record companies trusted each other. Eventually printed replicas of stamps became acceptable to both sides. Neither the 1911 Act nor the 1956 one contained provisions to allow the system of stamps to be short-circuited, so the fact that such short-circuiting eventually became feasible was a tribute to the maturity of the industry. Nowadays record companies use impeccable accounting techniques, assisted by computers, to calculate the royalties for composers. Modern mass-produced media such as cassettes or compact discs could never be marketed if each one had to carry a stamp.

Most record companies had standard label designs which were printed in large quantities, while the details specific to the actual issue in question were overprinted using one colour of ink. Thus an unusual design for a specific record adds to the interest, and sometimes to the value (**33**).

In 1908 the Gramophone Company received the Royal Warrant, which named them suppliers of records and record-players to the British Royal Family. And in 1923 the company made the first published record by a reigning British monarch, King George V and Queen Mary's 'Empire Day Message to the Boys and Girls of the British Empire' (**34**). Now the company faced a dilemma. Such records justified being at the top of the class structure, with heaven

a

b

c

d

33 (a to d) Unusual labels. These records were given conventional catalogue numbers and were sold at normal prices, but they have special label designs.

34 The first record by a reigning British Monarch.

knows what colour of label; but this would be undemocratic. They decided to price it in the middle of the range, at the 'black label' level, but they issued the actual record with a special Royal Purple design. Wireless broadcasting was unable to cover the Empire in 1923. There was no other way for the boys and girls of the British Empire to hear the speech, so local schools were obliged to buy copies, and there was much criticism of the cost. Most subsequent Royal records were therefore issued in the cheap 'plum label' series, although always decorated with special designs.

It was normal practice for the trademark to occupy the upper half of the design, while the title and other details occupied the lower half. The exceptions are sufficiently rare to be worth a study on their own;

35 'Triangle centre' record (Brunswick 45-05688).

it was quite a challenge for designers to make effective use of a relatively small circular area with a hole in the middle. The challenge became even greater with the advent of 45rpm discs, which had to be provided with an 'optional centre' no less than an inch and a half in diameter for quick-acting autochange and juke-box mechanisms. Designers therefore could not use the middle of the label to carry vital information.

It is not so much the label which affects the collectability of early rock records, but the nature of this 'optional centre'. Until 1957 the Decca group in Great Britain made a detachable piece in the shape of a triangle (35). These 'triangle centres' tend to fetch high prices among collectors, because they are pretty safe guarantees that the disc in question was actually manufactured during the golden years of rock 'n' roll, and is not a more modern pressing. There is a similar consideration for products of Britain's other principal manufacturer, the EMI group. Its earliest singles had labels printed with gold ink; these, too, tend to have a higher value than later equivalents printed in silver.

In 1975 the Polygram group of companies reverted to the old idea of paperless 'labels' for its ordinary seven-inch singles (36). The new process used injection-moulding rather than compression-moulding. The equipment could work faster, the mould was sealed against the ingress of dirt, and it was no longer necessary to provide paper labels.

By the 1970s record manufacturers seemed to be forming new logos (or trade-names) as fast as they could, and the entry of hundreds

36 A paperless label, used on seven-inch singles from 1975 onwards, in a surprising reversion to Berliner's technique.

of small independent companies added to the confusion. Some companies deliberately parodied the new trade-names, safe in the knowledge they would never be taken seriously. Thus 'Scratchy Records', 'Some Bizarre Records', and 'What Records?' appeared. And it became fashionable to market records in various editions, with alternative sound mixes and different lengths, editions pressed on coloured vinyl, editions incorporating pictures, and editions in funny shapes.

All of these developments detracted from the label as a source of interest in its own right, and the charm of classic record labels is increasingly unrecognised by collectors.

Fakes and forgeries

Before the days of portable recording machines which everyone could carry with them, record companies had to use great imagination to fill their catalogues with new and interesting material. It is fascinating to study the way that they bent the truth to promote a saleable product, yet even if the Trades Descriptions Act had been in force then, they would hardly ever have broken the law. It is interesting to see how close to the wind they sailed; the results have lessons for collectors today.

To be fair, the very earliest examples of misrepresentation were considered normal practice by the artists themselves. Before the days of audiences counted in millions, it was quite acceptable for artists to imitate other artists. One example which comes to mind is Bransby Williams, who emulated the performances of Charles Dickens and Sir Henry Irving throughout the first half of this century. In the late 19th century it was apparently a normal party-piece to imitate a well-known literary figure, signing-off with the name of the victim; this has caused some confusion today, where recordings 'signed off' by Sir Henry Irving and Oscar Wilde now have their authenticity questioned.

In the case of Oscar Wilde there is very good reason for doubt. To start with, nobody seems to have seen the original cylinder, which was supposed to have been recorded when Wilde visited an exhibition in Paris in the year 1900. Connoisseurs who heard tape copies were also suspicious of the vocal mannerisms; but engineers at the National Sound Archive were able to declare it a forgery the moment they heard it, for an unassailable technical reason. The surface-noise has a narrower frequency range than the speech. This simply cannot happen, unless the speech and the surface-noise came from two different sources. There are other dubious points too, but that one is conclusive.

Prime Minister William Gladstone is another well-known figure whose speeches have been 'discovered' from time to time recorded on cylinders. The majority of these were made by the London firm which, after various legal problems and takeovers, became Edison-Bell. The recordings comprise passages read from written accounts of parliamentary speeches by William Lynd, who made a living in the early 1890s by demonstrating and lecturing on the phonograph. Although a primitive recording programme was in progress, the company evidently had to scrape the bottom of the barrel for material. As we saw earlier, cylinders were individually made and carried no labels at that time, so it is understandable that mistakes occur nowadays when the only evidence is that of the recording itself.

However, William Gladstone *is* known to have recorded cylinders for Colonel Gouraud, an associate of Edison's in London. Colonel Gouraud was a social climber, who found the phonograph a perfect excuse to fraternize with high society in England (37). Gladstone was

37 Little Menlo. From his house in south London, called 'Little Menlo' after Edison's laboratory at Menlo Park in America, Colonel Gouraud promoted the works of the great inventor. He and his assistants captured the voices of many famous people during the Victorian era.

only one of many people whom he persuaded to record — in this case, a message congratulating Edison upon his invention. But there are at least two different versions in existence, plus some dubbings and several forgeries. The first was, according to the autobiography of Rowland Prothero (a guest present at the time), 'an eloquent and lengthy speech on the new link between England and America, delivered with such fire that no one noticed that the cylinder was exhausted half way, and that the needle was rotating in mid-air. The calamity was discovered after he left, and the next morning he gave a totally different and even more eloquent record to Edison's enterprising representative, Colonel Gouraud'. The first is probably the one copied by the BBC Sound Archive in 1935; at any rate, it comprises only the first three sentences. In March 1938 the BBC played this copy to some of Mr. Gladstone's friends and relations, and they confirmed it was 'probably genuine'. As for the 'totally different' recording mentioned by Prothero, that seems to have vanished; but a third version was definitely recorded by Gladstone at a later date, and sent to Edison:

Dear Mr. Edison,
I am profoundly indebted to you for, not the entertainment only, but the instruction and the marvels of one of the most remarkable evenings which it has been my privilege to enjoy. The request that you have done me the honour to make, to receive the record of my voice, is one that I cheerfully

comply with so far as lies in my power; though I lament to say that the voice which I transmit to you is only the relic of an organ the employment of which has been overstrained. Yet I offer to you as much as I possess, and so much as old age has left me, with the utmost satisfaction, as being at least a testimony to the instruction and delight that I have received from your marvellous invention. As to the future consequences: it is impossible to anticipate them. All I see is that wonders upon wonders are opening before us. Your great country is leading the way in the important work of invention. Heartily do we wish it well; and to you, as one of its greatest celebrities, allow me to offer my hearty good wishes and earnest prayers that you may long live to witness its triumphs in all that appertains to the well-being of mankind. William Ewart Gladstone

When commercial record-making got under way, deceptions became more tortuous. One such example is to be found in the 1905 Columbia Disc Record catalogue (**38**). Record No. 833 is titled: 'Address by the Late President McKinley at the Pan-American Exposition'. Actually, it is not President McKinley performing, but the catalogue does not claim that it is. Reading between the lines it

38 From the Columbia catalogue of 1905.

67

Disc number with no mark indicates 7-in. and 10-in.
*preceding disc number indicates 10-in. only.
†preceding disc number indicates 7-in. only.

Miscellaneous

833	Address by the Late President McKinley at the Pan-American Exposition
851	Dissertation on Love
†854	Football Match
855	How I Got to Morrow
296	How Rogers Brothers Play Golf
160	Lincoln's Speech at Gettysburg
162	Little Red Riding Hood
35	Negro Sermon, A
844	On Mutton Pies
845	On Sweethearts
847	On Trousers
850	Political Meeting, A
34	Stump Speech on Love
664	Twenty-third Psalm, and the Lord's Prayer, The
849	Women's Rights Meeting

Dutch Dialect Series

†26	Schultz on the Man Behind the Gun
28	Schultz on Christian Science
24	Schultz on George Washington
23	Schultz on Kissing
25	Schultz on Malaria
27	Schultz's Trip to Chicago

By Joseph Jefferson

*1469	Rip Meets Meenie after Twenty Years Absence (from "Rip Van Winkle")
*1468	Scene in the Mountain (from Second Act, "Rip Van Winkle")

Uncle Josh Weathersby's Laughing Stories

70	Arrival in New York. Uncle Josh's
1518	Automobile, Uncle Josh on an (a new one by Stewart. Very laughable. Bound to be a seller)
1506	Baptizing at Hickory Corners Church, Uncle Josh at a
71	Base Ball Game, Uncle Josh at a
72	Bicycle, Uncle Josh on a
1408	Camp Meeting, Uncle Josh at a
1490	Chinese Laundry, Uncle Josh in a

Our records can be used on ANY MAKE of disc talking machine.

39 Coronation record, 1911.

40 Not stereophonic! André Previn is now better known as an orchestral conductor.

becomes clear that it is the address which was recorded, in a studio re-creation to cash in on the President's assassination.

There are numerous examples of tricks like this. Even the highest-priced leading manufacturer was not immune to these practices. 'His Master's Voice' 09253 (**39**) is labelled: 'Descriptive Coronation Record. Heard during the Royal Progress through London, on June 23rd 1911'. As we saw earlier, the technology of the time certainly could not have coped with a live street recording, so one wonders how the company got away with that. It turns out that the recording was made nearly a month before the procession, and a contemporary advertisement shows that the *record* was heard during the Royal Progress through London on 23 June. The small print makes it clear that the waiting crowds were in fact entertained by an 'Auxetophone' amplified gramophone.

The technology of sound recording has also attracted hype. The classic story is that of the blues singer Ma Rainey, contracted to a company which did not have electrical recording when it became publicized in 1926. Nevertheless, the company advertised one of Ma Rainey's records as having been 'electrically recorded'. When customers complained, they were blithely informed that while Ma Rainey sang, an electric light had been switched on in the studio. However, recent research has shown that this particular anecdote is unsubstantiated.

New technology means new vocabularies, and often old vocabularies are adapted for the new purpose. 'Electrically Recorded' is one such example. 'Stereo' is another; it was some time before the word had settled down to its present meaning, and American Columbia are not to be castigated for marking their 1953 seven-inch LPs with the word (**40**). This was before the days of two-channel stereo records, and the label simply meant to imply that there was spaciousness in the sound on the record. Deception was inadvertently assisted by the British Standards Institution in 1960, when they recommended that all records with a vertical element in the groove modulation should have the word 'Stereo' on the label. This was done with the best of intentions, to stop consumers damaging such records with mono pickups, but it opened the floodgates to many types of fake-stereo records in the following decades.

The 1970s was the decade of 'Quadraphonic' sound. The idea was to sit the listener in the middle of a square array of loudspeakers, so sound would come at him from all corners — despite the fact that most live performances of music take place in front of the listener. Most consumers had bought stereo equipment by then, and equipment manufacturers saw quadraphony as a golden opportunity to cash in on sales of new records, pickups, amplifiers, and loudspeakers. Much effort was expended in squeezing four channels of sound onto an LP disc, and there were four incompatible systems, none of which

41 (**a** and **b**)
Advertisements from 1925.
The one on the left
promotes a genuine
electrical recording success;
the one on the right
attempts to capitalize on it,
although recorded
acoustically.

worked very well. There seemed to be two areas of subject-matter where quadraphonics might have an artistic advantage, drama and wildlife recording, so it seemed very sensible when the first 'quadra-phonic' record of birdsong was announced. However, it was not possible to get any quadraphonic effect from the record, no matter which system was tried. I later interviewed the bemused recordist, and established he had been given two portable stereo tape recorders, which he had laid on the ground pointing in opposite directions. The two unsynchronized tapes were then simply mixed together back at base before being transferred to disc. This explained why it had not been possible to get four separate channels of sound out of the record.

One of the first genuine electrical recordings was *Adeste Fideles* sung in the Metropolitan Opera House New York by the choir of the Associated Glee Clubs of America (850 voices), before an audience of 4000. The audience joined in the last verse, inspiring Columbia to claim that their record had 4850 voices on it (**41a**). This is doubtful for a start; but the English Edison Bell Company went one better —

literally. In 1925 they published a 'descriptive' record entitled 'Mr and Mrs Brown at the Football Match', claiming 4851 voices could be heard. Actually there were probably fewer than twenty, but purchasers were assured the claim could only be verified by listening to the record and counting for themselves (**41b**).

Despite the constant temptation to misuse an artist's name, there seem to be very few cases where the customer was actually deceived, although this surely must have happened with some pirate or bootleg records. Top performers jealously protected themselves from all types of misrepresentation, so it is hardly surprising that record companies didn't try it on. One case which comes close to misrepresentation is English Columbia's recording of the *Introduction and Allegro* by Ravel, recorded in late 1923, which was alleged to be 'conducted' by the composer. Apart from the question of whether seven top (named) instrumentalists would submit to being 'conducted' in a chamber work at all, there is the point that, by all accounts, Maurice Ravel was not a good conductor. It is actually a very good performance of the

42 Which copy of this 1955 record by Elvis is original, and which is a forgery? A genuine one always has three tiny depressions one-quarter of an inch in diameter close to the centre-hole. (You need oblique light to show them; there is one beneath the bottom right of the letter U of SUN, for example). This is because the original master-lacquer had three extra drive-holes, which had to be filled in before the stampers could be made. Master-lacquers don't normally have extra drive-holes, and this point was missed by the first forgers. But since then, other forgeries have appeared complete with drive-hole marks.

piece, so it is possible to conclude that Ravel was present only in an advisory capacity, if at all. The deception, if deception it was, errs on the right side.

In most other similar cases, the label does specifically say 'Recorded in the presence of. . . ' or 'Recorded under the supervision of. . . ', with only one minor exception. The Gramophone Company's record-producer Fred Gaisberg had the idea of carrying out a recording session 'supervised' by Sir Edward Elgar, then lying upon his deathbed in Worcestershire. On 22 January 1934 'His Master's Voice' arranged for his house to be connected to the London studio by landlines. When *Dream Children* (Opus 43) was issued, the label said 'Recorded under the supervision of Sir Edward Elgar'. In his definitive book *Elgar On Record,* Jerrold Northrop Moore says that this item was recorded before the landlines were working; but the 'Woodland Interlude' from *Caractacus* was recorded under his supervision and this item plus the first half of *Dream Children* was later copied onto the same side for publication.

In February 1953 EMI issued their complete recording of Wagner's *Tristan und Isolde* conducted by Furtwangler. A year later there was a sensation in the newspapers, when an EMI employee revealed that the ageing Kirsten Flagstad's top Cs in the love duet in Act II had been sung for her by Elisabeth Schwarzkopf. This seems mild enough compared to the everyday manipulation of today's multi-track techniques; but it is the exception which proves the rule. The row, about just two notes in over four hours of music, illustrates just how careful the recording industry had been to attribute correctly its big names until then.

The question of claimed artists does not, of course, apply to deliberate '*noms-du-disque*', which were extremely frequent in the old days, and the technique is not dead yet. As with Ravel, the deception was usually in favour of the consumer, because it often turned out to be a famous and justly well-known artist using a different name for contractual reasons. Sometimes the pseudonyms were ludicrous, such as 'Arty Chuckles', 'R. T. Goodfellow', and 'B. Gay' for the laughing comedian Charles Penrose.

Most pseudonyms were less self-evident. It would take many pages to list all the ones which have been identified by researchers today, but the phenomenon was not just confined to recordings. The artists themselves sometimes had a Jekyll-and-Hyde career, the prime example being the Australian bass-baritone Peter Dawson, who for many years dressed up as a Scotsman and hijacked Sir Harry Lauder's songs, touring Scottish music-halls under the name Hector Grant. He was evidently so successful at 'carrying the coals to Newcastle', making a ten-year career out of the impersonation and rerecording Sir Harry's repertoire for Sir Harry's record company, that when the pair met at the recording studio in 1920 and their producer told Sir Harry about the deception, he simply refused to believe it.

Another form of deception which affected the consumer occurred in the early days of LPs. Composers and publishers of songs were rewarded with royalties upon the sale of each record, but some companies hit upon the idea of renaming songs, and claiming that the record company (or some associated concern) had published them. They evidently worked on the assumption that no one at the Mechanical Copyright Protection Society ever actually listened to the records. However, since in this situation customers never knew what they were buying, the scheme didn't last very long.

Alas, the biggest deceptions in gramophone history comprised serious music, which was for many years 'cut down', both in duration and instrumentation. The first symphony to be recorded was Schubert's *Unfinished,* published on one twelve-inch disc by American Columbia in 1911. Fortuitously, its very title makes the short version acceptable under the Trades Descriptions Act! But for the next decade or more, nearly all orchestral and instrumental music was issued in cut-down form, without any warning being given. As violinist Mischa Elman said after recording an excerpt from Gounod's *Faust,* 'it will do, but it is not *Faust* — it is *Faust* de-composed!' As recently as 1952 the British Decca Company was advertising Gilbert and Sullivan in 'complete long-playing recordings by the D'Oyly Carte Opera Company'. Musically this is very nearly correct, but not one recording includes so much as a single word of Gilbert's spoken dialogue.

The market for fakes and forgeries is, of course, fuelled by money, and the recent rise in prices in some areas of record collecting has increased the trend. The first examples to appear were facsimilies of Elvis Presley's first records for the 'Sun' label. The originals were

43 Lionel Mapelson, photographed backstage at the Metropolitan Opera House, New York. Using this giant horn, he captured live operatic performances on cylinders during the years 1900 - 1902.

made before his contract was acquired by RCA Victor. Presley made five records for 'Sun', each of which was issued in 78rpm and 45rpm versions. Despite his death, Elvis Presley has, more than any other artist, a large — even growing — fan club. Each genuine 'Sun' record is worth about three hundred pounds to a collector aiming to acquire all of Elvis's records. In this case, the demand greatly exceeds the supply, and facsimiles of the 45rpm versions were manufactured in 1972. Although these were originally marketed specifically as facsimiles, few collectors have ever seen an original 'Sun', and they have since tended to change hands as if they were genuine (**42**). Even this did not fulfill the demand, and there are now much better forgeries, which even include the 78rpm versions. To ensure the right chemical composition for these (shellac not being available nowadays), forgers have bought up supplies of less desirable genuine 'Sun' records and recycled them. Nevertheless, the problems of reactivating obsolete technology are not confined to 78s. A bootlegger known as 'Ace' in California has even made pretty accurate copies of three British ten-inch LPs of Elvis's material issued by His Master's Voice, including their sleeves with their peculiar cellophane coating.

It is difficult to appreciate the logic of these reproductions. A sound archivist will want a recording which gets close to the sound of the original master-tape. The rights to Presley's 'Sun' recordings were acquired by RCA Victor together with the rights to the artist, and although it is now known that the tapes in RCA Victor's vault are not actually the 1955 originals, they are extremely good copies, and all have been reissued on compact disc. Thus collectors can get back to the sound of the original master-tape far more closely than would be possible with any 1955 disc, let alone a forgery of one.

There are very few artists whose genuine records attract prices which justify forgeries. In 1987 the 'Black Album' of pop singer Prince was withdrawn before it was issued, and only a few genuine copies 'escaped'. Andy Linehan, curator of pop music at the National Sound Archive, pointed out that, in one forged edition at least, the forgery was spotted because of a mistake in the small print round the label edge, which included the word 'outiside'. In this case the circumstances were peculiarly favourable for a forgery to be worthwhile. Many of Prince's records had attracted publicity for their sexual lyrics, and the circumstances of the record's withdrawal added fuel to the fire. The 'Black Album', being a pure black sleeve (apart from lettering on the spine), was also particularly easy to reproduce.

There are three records which have defied the searches of record-collectors, and since no one alive today has examples to compare them with, they would seem to be prime candidates for potential forgers. Two were scheduled for issue as Fonotipia 69000 and 69001, single-sided discs nearly fourteen inches across. They comprised two operatic arias sung by the tenor Jean de Reszke, which are known to have been recorded in Paris on 22nd April 1905. It is assumed that de Reszke was dissatisfied with test-pressings; at any rate, neither was issued. Another theory is that it was an engineering disaster; several other Paris recordings from the period are thin and distorted. Rumours got around that a collector in Paris had one in a bank vault in the 1940s; but this story was recently investigated, and was found to be based on a misunderstanding. A disc with a genuine de Reszke label is known, but it is attached to the wrong record! A test-pressing also survives in which Jean de Reszke accompanies his wife Marie on the piano (not very well, by all accounts). And the manager of the Metropolitan Opera House in New York, Lionel Mapleson (43), attempted some phonograph cylinders of live performances involving artists like Jean de Reszke. Many of these have survived, but the quality is so poor that one can't get much from them. The loss to posterity is incalculable. Jean de Reszke was probably the leading tenor of the 'Golden Age' of operatic singing, and all the written accounts of his work agree that his sense of drama was equal to that of his vocal talents. Collectors would give anything for the chance to hear him project his art to us from the clarity of a recording studio. The BBC series 'Revolutions in Sound', broadcast in 1988, gave great publicity to the possibility of these records existing, but nothing has so far turned up.

Another disc which has vanished (although many people actually remember it) is a slow rhythm-and-blues number published in America in 1952. It is Jubilee 5104, 'Stormy Weather' by the Five Sharps. The master was lost in a fire, no one can put their hands on a pressing, Jubilee does not even have a test copy, and nobody has a tape of it. This is a classic case which shows the advantage of the existence of an independent sound archive, perhaps government-backed to ensure it doesn't fall foul of copyright laws. It seems impossible for a well-selling pop record to vanish from the face of the earth, but it actually seems to have happened here.

The above non-existent records are, as I say, obvious candidates for forgery, but the simple fact of their being made by obsolete technology makes it less likely that forgeries will appear. There would have to be a high potential return to justify the trouble and expense. 'Acetate' discs were, for many years, the equivalent of wax cylinders before magnetic tape became universal. They were used by pro-fessionals and keen amateurs whenever a small number of tailor-made discs were required. I consider the most likely candidate for forgery is therefore an unknown cylinder or an unknown acetate disc — in other words, a one-off, which would be difficult to compare with the genuine article, because there would be nothing with which to compare it. In this field the first 'acetate' made by The Beatles was recently bought back by Paul McCartney, reportedly for £10,000. The disc went missing for many years, and was the subject of at least one book. Some collectors thought it would be the most valuable recording known to exist. (The 'Golden Disc' of The Beatles' 'Sergeant Pepper' was auctioned in 1982 for £14,300, but of course that wasn't the only copy of the recording in existence).

What would be the next most valuable 'one-off'? In cultural terms, it would probably be a recording by George Orwell, author of *1984* and *Animal Farm*. George Orwell wrote for the BBC Overseas Service and made hundreds of radio broadcasts, but no recording of his voice seems to have survived anywhere. It forms what is probably the most serious gap in the BBC's (and this nation's) sound archives.

Freaks and follies

'Standardization' is an issue which has plagued engineers for years. This is because the engineer's role is a dual one. First, he has to make scientific discoveries actually work, and second, he has to do it cost-effectively. He uses scientific methodology for both processes — forming hypotheses, testing them, and going back to the drawing board. In the process, the balance between his two purposes - making something work, and making it cheaply — often becomes confused. The issue is even more complicated in the world of sound recording, because we cannot pick up a record and listen to it in the same way that we can pick up a book and read it. Technical apparatus of some sort has to come between the record and our ears, and, of course, between the original performance and the record. And as new scientific principles combine with new economic and artistic factors, the nature of the record in the middle has to change. This results in problems of standardization.

Obviously, evolution must continue to take place if artistic, technical, and economic progress is to be made. Yet sound engineers often wish the process would stop for a while, so they can catch their breath and rationalize the many-headed monster they have created. The only relief is that some of the heads wither away as new ideas take over, so that old techniques and formats become redundant. Progress cannot be made without exploring blind alleys. So, although we may wish that the monster would stop sprouting new heads, it is entertaining to look at some of the blind alleys of the past, most of which were investigated quite seriously at the time.

Conventional Cylinders

Edison's tinfoil phonograph could record only about one minute of speech, and his wax phonograph of 1887 could accommodate 'about two hundred words'. This was at a time when cylinders were only used for dictation purposes, not for recording music, and a speed of about 100 revolutions per minute was found adequate. But music, with a wider frequency range than speech, required the cylinder to turn faster (giving a shorter playing-time). The resourceful advertisers made a virtue out of this necessity. Columbia's 'X-P High-Speed' cylinders ran at 160rpm, and this fact was pushed for all it was worth. The playing-time was almost exactly two minutes, and such 'two-minute cylinders' became standard for commercial prerecorded fare, while 100rpm remained more or less standard for dictation cylinders and privately-made cylinders recorded in the home.

That is the theory. In practice, all types of cylinders could vary widely. The fastest prerecorded cylinders were probably those produced by the French Pathé company; some of these are known to turn at over 200rpm.

Recently, I was faced with the task of transferring a set of thirty lessons of Britain's first commercial language course, the Linguaphone French course of 1906, onto tape. They were recorded on 'moulded' cylinders, not wax, so I was not surprised when the first one gave sensible sounds at the conventional speed. But as I continued, it became apparent that the course planners were having increasing difficulty in getting each lesson on to one cylinder. By Lesson 27 the speed had dropped to 87rpm, the speed I had to use to get the voice to sound the same as Lesson 1. So I will claim this to be the lowest speed of any commercial prerecorded 'two-minute' cylinder, which ran for the best part of four minutes now.

There are only two other ways the playing-time could have been increased. One was to make the grooves finer, so more could be packed in the same space; and the other was to increase the size of the cylinder. Edison himself followed both principles. The first principle was put into effect in 1908. Until then all cylinders had one hundred 'lines per inch'; that is, the cylinder rotated one hundred times while the mouthpiece moved along one inch. It was not possible to vary this, because playback machines had to have a similar gearing mechanism. But when Edison introduced his 'Amberol' cylinders, they had 200 lines per inch. Inexpensive conversion-kits were made available for many Edison models of phonograph, and the new 'four-minute' cylinders remained in production until 1929. In 1912 Edison introduced the compatible 'Blue Amberol' records made of an even tougher plastic; and it is generally accepted that Blue Amberols had a better, higher fidelity performance than any other medium before the First World War.

The other principle, bigger cylinders, was less successful, mainly because existing phonographs could not cope with it. The longest prerecorded cylinders regularly marketed bore the legend 'Smethurst's System', and were made by the Sterling company in London. They were four-and-three-quarter inches long, and would fit onto most machines, but gave only a few seconds extra time. But, for the office dictation market, Edison made machines to cut cylinders six inches long with a compromise pitch of 150 lines per inch. Compatability with existing phonographs did not matter, because dictation cylinders rotated at a different speed anyway. The 'Edison Voicewriter' machine remained in use for well over half a century (**45**). Unlike modern tape systems, it was possible to jump backwards and play a word again quickly if it wasn't clear. The BBC Monitoring Service used them for deciphering 'jammed' radio broadcasts, and my solicitor, at least, was still dictating into an Edison Voicewriter in 1973.

Unconventional Cylinders

Many inventors attempted to buck the system by making alterations to existing machinery. In retrospect, one often wonders how they thought they could possibly succeed. One 'Longest Playing Phone' of

44 Longest-playing phone. A machine dating from 1908 which was designed to give eight minutes of reproduction from cylinder records.

1908 (**44**) used cylinders sixteen inches long. Actually, close examination shows these comprised four four-inch cylinders. So although the machine may have run for eight minutes, it was not an uninterrupted eight minutes. Imagine the appalling noises as the stylus crossed from one cylinder to the next. So you will search in vain for any sixteen-inch cylinders today.

The 'Lioretograph' cylinders were invented by the Frenchman Lioret as early as 1897. They were quite small with a celluloid surface. Hot water was used to soften the material before it was cut, so it took the undulations at full volume, and there was a very large soundbox for replay, so the system was louder than its competitors (**46** — see also page 4). But the cylinders were so small they could not hold more than a minute of material. The surviving records and machines sound very good; but why such a tiny cylinder? Inevitably, Lioretographs disappeared within three or four years.

At the Paris exhibition of 1900 (the one at which Oscar Wilde is supposed to have been recorded), the Columbia company introduced their 'Multiplex Grand' machine, using a giant cylinder played by three styli and horns. We can see from (**47**) that the cylinder had three soundtracks side-by-side; presumably it was recorded by three cutters side-by-side, in which case the record would have stereophonic

45 The Edison 'Voice Writer' machine. Designed for office dictation use, this machine followed Edison's preferred method of using electricity for the motor, but it had acoustic recording and reproduction.

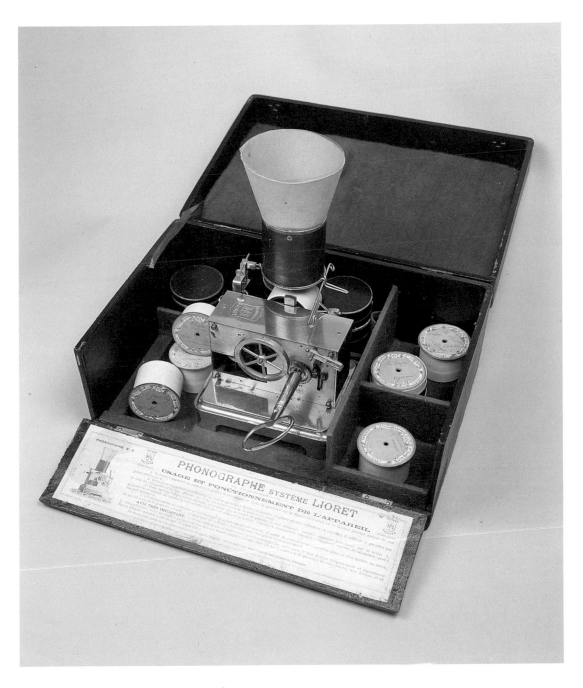

46 A Lioretograph.

47 The Columbia Multiplex Grand Phonograph.

properties. When stereo LPs were launched in 1958, someone pointed out this fact, and research was put in motion to find out what had happened to the 'stereo cylinder'. It was found that the machine had been purchased by a Sultan in the Middle East, but its whereabouts could not be discovered. It seems that the Sultan was one of the first victims of non-standardization; he paid a thousand dollars for a machine for which only one cylinder was ever made!

Longer-Playing Recordings

Three factors (size, speed, and groove-pitch) might be manipulated to make long-playing records. And because discs were on the market for a longer time, and attracted more investment, there are a correspondingly large number of 'freaks' around. Probably the first long-playing disc records were made by the Neophone Company of London in 1904; they were twenty inches in diameter. The recordings comprised uninterrupted performances of opera overtures, but they cost ten shillings and sixpence each, and needed an outsize turntable. So customers spent their money on twelve-inch discs instead, and in fact I have never seen a twenty-inch Neophone record.

The 'Marathon' discs of 1912 (**48**) were made in the usual ten-inch and twelve-inch diameters, but with finer grooves. The idea was to record using 'hill-and-dale' modulation, with the grooves packed closer together because there would be no risk of overlap. In fact, the British inventor P. J. Packman took the idea a stage further; he developed a cutter for V-shaped grooves, rather than the U-shaped grooves then considered normal, so he got a deeper groove at the same time. This invention turned out to be ahead of its time; U-shaped grooves remained normal until 1939, and Packman-type cutters only became universal after the Second World War. One twelve-inch

48 Advertisement for
Marathon records.

Marathon record achieved a playing-time of more than 16 minutes,
spread over two sides; but customers had to change the soundbox of
their record-players to cope with 'hill-and-dale' grooves, and within
a couple of years non-standardization had claimed another victim.

Thomas Edison saw that the public were deserting cylinder records
for discs, so he announced his 'Diamond Disc Phonograph' in 1911,
although it was not ready until 1913. The new discs were also
hill-and-dale, recorded with a relatively fine groove-pitch of 150 lines
per inch, so a ten-inch side played rather longer than usual (about five
minutes). The grooves were U-bottomed with a radius of precisely 4.7
thousandths of an inch, and his reproducers were fitted with the very

49 World record controller. This is the mechanism on the left of the picture. In this case, it has been fitted to an HMV Gramophone; it controls the rotational speed of the disc so it runs slowly when the soundbox is at the outside edge, and allows the record to speed up towards the inner radius.

first diamond styli, of exactly this size for minimum wear and surface-noise. But the grooves were very shallow by normal disc standards, and to reduce the chances of the stylus being thrown out of the groove, the records were made absolutely flat, and a full quarter of an inch thick so they would be sure to stay that way. They turned out to be practically unbreakable as well as hard-wearing. When I visited the Edison National Historic Site a few years ago, my guide told me that the full resources of his employer (the United States Government) had failed to break one; but to find out exactly what was inside the quarter-inch slab, they had borrowed a diamond saw and cut one in half. He showed us the section, which comprised a core based on woodflour and phenol resin, while the surface was a more advanced phenolic resin applied to the face of the core in the form of 'Condensite varnish' stamped within the record press. He added that the phenol compounds were imported from Germany until the First World War cut off the supplies, whereupon Edison almost single-handedly founded the US plastics industry.

The war also kept Edison's Diamond Discs from Europe, so they

50 A twenty-inch Pathé disc. This example plays for 3 minutes 10 seconds and weighs 2.2 kilograms.

are rather uncommon in Britain. But, being virtually indestructible, they do turn up, and they're as well-recorded as his Blue Amberol cylinders. In fact, Edison's salesmen organized public 'Tone Tests', in which Edison artists would perform live, alongside their recordings from the Diamond Disc catalogue. This proved to many people's satisfaction that Edison's 're-creation' was indistinguishable from the original. Unfortunately, Edison was not himself a musician, and the technology he fathered was never used for mass-producing serious musical records. Since 1910 he had been recording discs in London, and Raymond Wile's list of Edison Disc Masters (published in the *Talking Machine Review* from August 1971 onwards) shows that many mouth-watering recordings of London opera-singers and other treasures were made. They were taken to America for mass-production. It seems, however, that everything Edison actually issued was American 'home-grown corn'.

Another long-playing disc was the 'World Record', invented in 1922 by Noel Pemberton-Billing. The principle was as follows. At the outside edge of a twelve-inch 78rpm record, the groove travels under the stylus at about 47 inches per second. At the end of the record, when the stylus is approaching the label, the groove is travelling at about twenty inches per second, yet the sound quality is very similar. Why not make the groove move at twenty inches per second throughout the whole disc? This means starting the record at about 33rpm, and speeding it up gradually as the stylus travels in. Pemberton-Billing's invention comprised an add-on governor mechanism which could be attached to a clockwork turntable to give this

51 Doll's House Disc. On this example, Peter Dawson's rendition of 'God Save The King' plays for 22 seconds. It weighs 200 milligrams.

effect (**49**), and a few dozen records were made which more than doubled the average playing-time. Within a couple of years, non-standardization had claimed another victim; but this time, the recorded legacy includes records which we cannot play back electronically, because the mechanism has to work with a clockwork motor. Alternatively, we could use an electronically–controlled variable-speed turntable, but we have no absolute way of knowing what the correct speed is. Fortunately 'World Records' seem to have few important recordings on them.

I wonder if Pemberton-Billing would be pleased if he could know that modern Laservision discs and Compact Digital Discs work on a similar principle, although starting in the middle and slowing down. On the new discs the material is recorded in batches called 'frames', and electronic circuitry counts the reproduced frames and controls the speed that way.

Louder Reproduction

Cylinders were also made in large diameters, with special machines to play them of course. The reason was not to give longer playing time, but to allow louder reproduction. Without amplification, cylinders could only be reproduced more loudly by altering the leverage between the stylus and the reproducing diaphragm. If the leverage was too high, the needle would not stay in the groove without the weight upon the point being increased. Bigger cylinders allowed this to happen without extra wear. But since all large commercially-made cylinders seem to have been copied from standard ones, there was no increase in quality, only in volume.

The principle that larger cylinders will withstand more wear can also be applied to discs. In 1909 the Pathé company, which had by then abandoned cylinders, made their own twenty-inch monsters. (50). They rotated at 120rpm, and they were intended to allow louder reproduction, not increased fidelity or playing-time. The groove was very coarse, and was played with a sapphire 32-thousandths of an inch in diameter. (Modern LP styli are around half a thousandth of an inch). The large stylus ensured there was a large area of contact, so large amounts of energy could be transmitted to the diaphragm without wear. But nothing was issued on the format which was not also available on smaller records. Apparently they were used in restaurants, skating-rinks, and similar venues.

The other extreme is represented by the special records made for Queen Mary's Doll's House exhibited at the Wembley Exhibition of 1924. Various representatives of British industry contributed miniature artefacts. The Gramophone Company supplied a tiny gramophone which really worked. In order to have something to play on it, the company made half-a-dozen special recordings which were pressed into tiny records an inch and five-sixteenths in diameter. Copies were sold to the public as souvenirs of the exhibition, and could be played on many contemporary record-players (51).

The quest for louder reproduction led to the first 'amplifying gramophones'. Early amplifiers were pneumatic, not electronic. A stream of compressed air was modulated by a shutter vibrated by the stylus, instead of a stream of electrons being modulated by voltages from a pickup. Such amplifiers needed a supply of compressed air, which might come from a hand-pump, an electric motor, or cylinders of compressed gas (52). It is reliably reported that such a machine could be heard five miles away. The Gramophone Company began marketing an attachment called 'The Auxetophone' in 1905. It was designed to play conventional records, so its existence is not apparent from record collections today.

Yet the evidence is there if we care to look for it. In those days there were no public-address systems, and the principle of the Auxetophone was the only way of producing loud speech. It is thought that the records made by British politicians before the General Election of January 1910 were played to voters by means of Auxetophones; certainly their expected sales would not have justified their production. It also seems Auxetophones account for the large numbers of records made by both candidates for the American Presidential Election of 1908, which were recorded by Victor, the Gramophone Company's American partner.

In 1921 Lord Northcliffe, the founder of the London newspaper the *Daily Mail,* was due to speak at a dinner for 3000 staff to celebrate the twenty-fifth birthday of the paper, but he had a throat infection,

52 Gramophone with Auxetophone attachment. This model has a hand-pump for the amplifier. Since the turntable had a clockwork winding mechanism and the air-pump demanded continuous cranking while the disc played, you had to be fit to play a record!

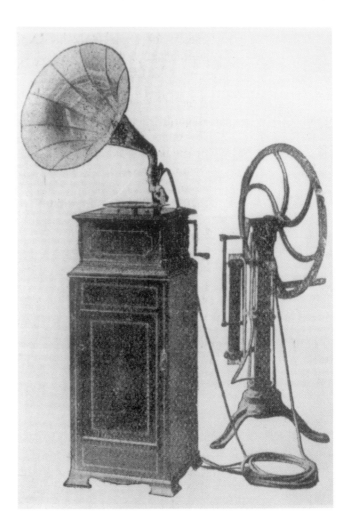

and his doctor advised him not to speak. Instead, he went to the Gramophone Company's factory at Hayes, and on 28 April he made a private record of the speech, proposing a toast to the future of the paper. On 4 May it was played through an Auxetophone to the diners so they could all hear his words. If the Auxetophone had not existed, we would not have a record of Lord Northcliffe's voice today.

The Auxetophone also permitted the first disc-copying to take place. It was impossible to transfer sound waves mechanically from one flat disc to another without getting into geometrical difficulties, and an ordinary gramophone was not loud enough to be put in front of an acoustic recording horn. But an Auxetophone was; and although the resulting records had a very poor frequency range, it was good enough for the voice of the quail. Quail-hunting was a popular sport in Italy. In 1913 the Gramophone Company copied seven seconds of Quail-song 29½ times (the half being when the operator, with muffled curses, misplaced the reproducing needle). The result was a record for Italian quail-hunters to lure birds to their doom with portable gramophones.

'Unbreakable' Records

The late 1920s and early 1930s were the days of the Unbreakable Record Craze. Conventional shellac records were very brittle; only a few ounces of shear stress would crack them in half. The first phase of the battle was to coat the shellac on a cardboard base; in fact, the Neophone Company of 1904 had tried this idea. By 1929 the Duophone Unbreakable Record Company had established a large factory to make similar records, the core of which was a thick slab of fibrous cardboard. The company also made records for the 'World-echo' and 'Siemens' labels, and they were given away as Christmas presents in giant Christmas crackers made by Mead & Fields Ltd. Although the records would withstand shear stresses, a simple knock on the edge could allow the two sides to be split apart. Discographer Brian Rust recalls playing one side of a record while holding the other in his hand, and he also adds that the cardboard formed the best blotting-paper imaginable! The company had to convert its vast new factory to making ordinary shellac records, which the copy-writers called 'solid', not 'breakable'. It became the factory of the newly-founded Decca Record Company within eighteen months.

The developing plastics industry encouraged new avenues of experimentation, three of which resulted in unbreakable records which all appeared in the year 1930. 'Filmophone' records were made of various colours of plastic, and had low surface-noise combined with great ruggedness; but within a short time they warped so badly that they were unplayable. Now archivists have to use a vacuum turntable to suck them flat. The Filmophone Company had a great deal of legal trouble with the British branch of another company, the German 'Phonycord GmbH'. Their records were very similar, except that they were all amber-coloured, and the only one I have seen is almost flat. 'Goodson' records were less badly afflicted by warping, but shrank instead. It does not really matter if a ten-inch record turns into a nine-and-a-half inch, but it does matter when the shrinkage is uneven, because the grooves become highly eccentric.

'Durium' records came nearest to success; the first appeared on 8 April 1932. The idea came from America, where the equivalent was called 'Hit of the Week'. Whereas the three unbreakable makes of 1930 were distributed by record shops in the usual way, you ordered your Durium records from your newsagent, so a pair of new hits were delivered through your letterbox once a week, like magazines (you could also buy them over the counter, of course). They combined the two features of flexibility and long-playing time. A relatively thin piece of cardboard — more like thick paper, really — was coated on one side with a material called 'Durium'. Because it was single-sided, the groove pitch was doubled to allow two numbers on each disc. The same company also made a French language course and many advertising mini-discs. Despite their apparent fragility, there are lots of examples surviving today, and collectors were genuinely sorry when the series came to a halt after only forty-two weeks. Durium records probably came nearest to making sound recordings really accessible to the masses, forming a gramophonic equivalent of the paper-backed book.

None of these unbreakable records succeeded in displacing shellac. Actually, shellac was perhaps the least important constituent; the most important was slate dust, whose abrasive and gritty properties were needed for a rather unusual reason. As we saw earlier, discs permitted simple and cheap record-players; but the advantage was lost if the record-players had to have sapphire or diamond points made out of precious gems. So steel needles were often used instead. To make the needle fit the groove, the disc contained abrasive material, so the tip would be ground down during the first two or three revolutions. This system remained until polyvinyl chloride records began to appear.

'Vinyl' was much more expensive. During the Second World War, many of the world's armies were in foreign lands, and countries had to send music and entertainment to their forces to keep up morale. Shellac records were simply too fragile to be posted; so the special circumstances of war justified the first vinyl records. Initially, they were filled with slate dust, so they could be played with ordinary heavyweight pickups. After the war, 'unfilled' vinyl was used because it had much less surface noise, and a few sets of unfilled vinyl 78s were made for early hi-fi buffs. But it was not until the development of the LP that the cost could be absorbed for the everyday consumer, because an LP could hold five times as much material. The shellac record disappeared about 1960, and nowadays all disc records are 'unbreakable' by comparison.

One cannot help wondering what future generations will think of *our* freaks and follies. As this book was going to press, an anonymous correspondent of *The Weekend Telegraph* wrote concerning the pop group House Of Love, whose single 'Shine On' had been re-recorded. Apart from the original version, the new performance was available as a video, a 7-inch single, a 12-inch single, a CD-single and a cassette single. The band was clearly appealing to 'completist' fans with a second 12-inch single with additional tracks and a second 4-track CD with further additional tracks. And those were just the British issues, which did not yet include a conventional album. Instead of joining up to defeat the many-headed monster I mentioned earlier, today's record collectors sometimes seem to be their own worst enemies.

The Five Senses

For a hundred years sound recordists have been claiming how perfectly their recordings represented the original. The expression 'High Fidelity' dates back to the 1930s, but the idea is much older. Admirers of Edison's tinfoil phonograph are on record as saying that it was impossible to tell the difference between the recording and the original.

How could this be? Well, before the invention of sound recording — and indeed for some time after — the only thing people could compare it with was stenography. In those days, shorthand writers formed the only means by which ordinary speech could be recorded, and it was as a substitute for the stenographer that the phonograph was first marketed. It was therefore natural to test the phonograph as if it were taking down shorthand. One conclusive test was conducted by an American bishop, suspicious that there might be a ventriloquist hidden behind a curtain. He recited a list of biblical names at high speed into the machine, expecting it to stumble and clear its throat. When it repeated the words back perfectly, the bishop claimed there was no human being in the world who could have done that, and the machine's fidelity was perfect.

Ever since then, people have been conducting tests upon different generations of sound recording systems. A complete survey of these would be a fascinating project for a doctorate in psychoacoustics. This

53 An unusual record combining the qualities of a 'picture disc' (on the back), with a special label design (on the front).

54 An Edison-Bell Picturegram of 1927, an early attempt at audio-visual entertainment. The record tells a story, complemented by a picture scroll. The machine was easy to damage and was not a huge success.

is because the nature of the mechanical deficiencies changed with time, and so did our predecessors' perceptions of them. Contemporary reports show that audiences often had difficulties appreciating various kinds of distortion if these distortions had no counterparts in real life. In the late 1950s, for example, listeners had to learn how to listen to stereo. The two microphone techniques mentioned earlier were then rivals, and professional engineers and amateurs could not easily switch from one to the other, much less judge absolute fidelity.

There is another dimension to the problem. Once people had become accustomed to the very idea of mechanically reproduced sound, they could not accept sudden large improvements in quality. This attitude is illustrated by a very old anecdote. As long ago as 1925, when the American Victor company was trying to decide whether to use the Western Electric recording system, Victor executives complained that 'it didn't sound like a phonograph'. But there was sometimes another logical reason for resisting change, although the people who proposed improvements could never admit it. Tests by the BBC Research Department in the 1940s showed listeners actually preferred restricted frequency-range reproduction, which was then normal on the radio. However, the published report made no mention of the fact that the earliest full-range loudspeakers were much inferior to the ones we have today. Having sweated to produce a loudspeaker capable of reproducing the full frequency range, the experimenters refused even to consider the possibility that the test subjects might be rebelling against some new form of distortion instead of appreciating the improvement.

With mono recordings, many experiments over the decades have attempted to prove that it is impossible to tell the difference between the original and a recording. I shall mention one from my own experience. In 1969 there was an argument in the BBC Film Unit in Bristol about whether our films were being supplied with faithful sound. This is a rather odd question to start with, because films specifically do *not* have 'natural' sound. But a professional narrator was hired one morning, and alternate lines of speech were recorded using the normal microphone and recorder. Some listeners (including the producer who had made the original complaint) came into the

55 An example of evocative advertising used to sell the Edison Amberola Phonograph (see also back cover).

THE DEAR OLD "HEART SONGS," PLAYED ON THE EDISON, RECALL TO GRANDMOTHER AND
GRANDFATHER THE DAYS WHEN THEY WERE YOUNG

control room with the narrator. The former were blindfolded, and turned around on the spot to scramble their sense of direction. The narrator took up a position to one side of the loudspeaker, and the listeners were challenged to guess which was which as alternate lines were delivered. They could not do it.

So within a hundred years, man learnt to make recordings of sound with sufficient fidelity to fool the human ear — at least, sounds that did not come from several different points in space at the same time. It is now worthwhile to see how well we are doing with recording the other senses. The classical 'five senses' are sight, hearing, touch, taste, and smell; but this is an oversimplification, because there are lots of others as well — for example, the sense of balance, the sense of temperature, and the senses our muscles give us as they move.

We have not yet succeeded in creating reliable reproduction of touch, taste or smell, although there have been a few experiments. They usually work best in conjunction with the two senses we *can* record, sound and sight. This is because it is thought the human brain is not preprogrammed to recognize all the senses separately, but learns to correlate them in childhood. Psychologists believe a new-born infant learns to combine what it picks up through its various senses as it lies wriggling in its pram. So we can use one sense to stimulate a reaction in another sensory area.

Cinema films are a good example of this. They occupy most of the field of view of the audience, which is also kept in the dark so there is little distraction. Under these conditions it is possible to reproduce the sight of going down a helter-skelter, and the audience feels it is falling, when in fact there is no movement at all. The principle was

56 An advertisement from *The Sound Waves* — demonstrating the dangers of distortion from using the wrong needle, or the benefits of being 'blown away' by use of the right needle !

WHY NOT PLAY YOUR RECORDS "SYMPATHETIC"—ALLY ?

A suggested argument for the Edison Bell Sympathetic Chromic Needle.
—*By courtesy*, "*Judge*," *New York*.

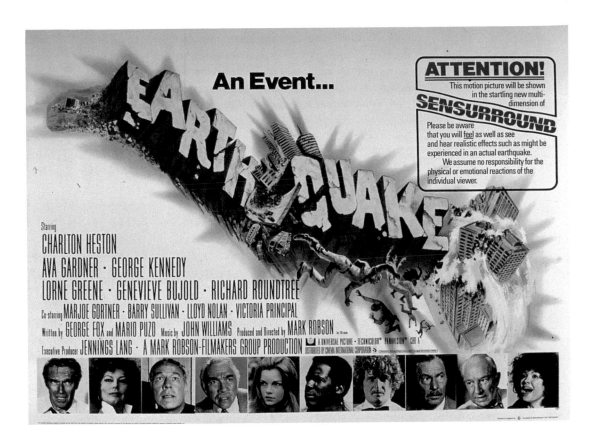

An Event...

ATTENTION!
This motion picture will be shown in the startling new multi-dimension of **SENSURROUND**

Please be aware that you will _feel_ as well as see and hear realistic effects such as might be experienced in an actual earthquake.

We assume no responsibility for the physical or emotional reactions of the individual viewer.

Starring
CHARLTON HESTON
AVA GARDNER · GEORGE KENNEDY
LORNE GREENE · GENEVIEVE BUJOLD · RICHARD ROUNDTREE
Co-starring MARJOE GORTNER · BARRY SULLIVAN · LLOYD NOLAN · VICTORIA PRINCIPAL
Written by GEORGE FOX and MARIO PUZO Music by JOHN WILLIAMS Produced and Directed by MARK ROBSON
Executive Producer JENNINGS LANG · A MARK ROBSON-FILMAKERS GROUP PRODUCTION A UNIVERSAL PICTURE · TECHNICOLOR® PANAVISION®

57 Sensationalist promotion of a new film and a new experience.

extended by the 'Sensurround' system (57). This was a powerful low-frequency sound system which blasted the audience with low-frequency pulses and physically shook them. In conjunction with suitably unsteady camerawork, the effect aimed to recreate the sensations of being in an earthquake; but as the majority of the movie audience had never experienced a real earthquake, it was difficult to assess the fidelity of the reproduction. The domination of the cinema screen over the audience has also resulted in experiments with 'smell-o-vision', but so far we have thankfully been spared Aldous Huxley's vision of 'the feelies'.

The only other sense man has had any success in recording and reproducing on its own is _sight_, although moving pictures and videos are a long way from fooling the human eye in quite the way sound can fool the ear. And when the senses of sight and sound are combined, it is usually necessary for the sound engineer to go through all sorts of contortions to make his recordings without upsetting the picture-recording process.

Most films are 'flat' — two-dimensional in other words. Over the decades film editors have built up a classical 'syntax' of editing, which circumvents the lack of three dimensions by showing the same scene from various viewpoints, rather in the way an observer will watch a conversation by switching his attention from one speaker to the other. As film viewers, we have learnt this 'grammar' subliminally, exactly as we learnt the grammar of language subliminally. Whenever the syntax is broken (for example, if the editor permits a 'jump-cut', or allows movement to 'cross the line', or allows a camera to 'zoom back' on objects which are coming closer), the viewer is disorientated. By developing this syntax, film editors replaced the lack of depth and all-round vision with something else. Taking the syntax for granted allows the construction of a new artistic edifice, rather in the way poetry builds upon the syntax of language. Thus we may have a close-up of a character weeping, viewed from a position in which, if the viewer were actually there, he would be coshed for intrusion of privacy. But we accept the syntax, and we are able to share the character's intimate emotions as a result.

The brain should never be given contradictory clues when we attempt to reproduce any of the senses. With stereoscopic photographs and films, for example, we get information about the disposition of objects in the scene partly from practical experience of the size of such objects, and partly from the differences between our two eyes. But we need other information to 'complete the picture'. In real life, we move our heads, and foreground objects appear to move in front of background objects because of parallax. The sense of balance is constantly giving our brains guidance about the way we are facing. The result with present 3-D pictures is that foreground objects tend to look flat — 'cut out of cardboard' is the common expression — because the viewer cannot look round an object by moving his head. The sense of balance is probably the most important one which should be harnessed by sound recording engineers. When it tells our brains which way our heads are pointing, it affects our perception of stereo and quadraphonic sound. You would think that the 'dummy head microphone' for 'binaural' reproduction — stereo sound for headphone listening — would give totally faithful stereo reproduction as a matter of principle. But it never quite works properly, because when the listener instinctively moves his head, the sound rotates as well. As this never happens in real life, many people find themselves assuming the sound must be behind the head.

We have no way of recording and replaying the sense of balance, and we can barely manage sight and sound with our present technology. So it is clear we have a long way to go before we can store up all the experiences of humankind. Yet sound will always be part of any future media, and I am pleased that sound recordings have reached such high technical and aesthetic standards after only one century of history.

Glossary

Acetate A term applied universally, but incorrectly, to a type of disc record in which the surface comprises cellulose nitrate lacquer, or occasionally gelatine, on a metal or glass base. In 1934 the inventor Cecil Watts found that cellulose nitrate could be soft enough for grooves to be cut, yet hard enough to withstand a few playings on any record-player, whilst also giving the lowest surface-noise of any recorded medium when new. 'Acetate' discs therefore became the ideal instantaneous sound recording medium for the next forty years, after which audio cassettes occupied their niche. 'Master acetates' also replaced wax for mass-production of pressings from about 1945 to 1980.

Acoustic recording A sound recording in which the vibrations of the cutter which recorded sound in a groove were obtained directly from the sound waves in the air. This type of recording always suffered from low sensitivity and a limited frequency response, so that only loud sounds could be recorded, and those only under controlled conditions.

Amberol cylinder Cylinder made by Thomas Edison's National Phonograph Company with a groove pitch of 200 turns per inch. The first Amberol cylinders were black and not particularly hard-wearing; but in 1912 the Blue Amberol cylinder was launched with very low surface noise and high resistance to wear. Purple Amberols were similar chemically, but denoted a more expensive Grand Opera-type recording.

Analog recording Form of recording medium whose characteristics vary in a manner which is analogous to the original. For example, with analog sound recording, when sound pressures increase, the strength of magnetism on a tape increases in proportion. The opposite of 'digital recording' (q v)

Auxetophone Acoustic reproducing machine marketed by The Gramophone Company about 1906-14, which incorporated a pneumatic amplifier to make the reproduction louder. There were similar machines by other makers.

Bias a) Signal mixed with the audio when recording on magnetic tape to reduce the distortion caused by the non-linear characteristics of permanent magnetic materials. 'Direct-current bias' was the oldest form, but because it left magnetized tape behind, even during silent passages, there was increased background noise. 'Alternating-current bias' is used nowadays, and consists of an ultrasonic signal which leaves demagnetised tape behind during silences, giving low distortion and low background noise.
b) When a conventional disc record is played with a pivoted arm correctly aligned, the friction between disc and stylus has the effect of pulling the arm inwards towards the centre of the record. This effect is neutralized on top-of-the-range systems by 'bias' mechanisms; the commonest type is a small weight attached to nylon cord running over a pulley.

Binaural recording In the 1930s to 1950s this term was synonymous with 'stereophonic recording', but more recently it has come to mean a recording specifically made to be heard on headphones, as opposed to loudspeakers.

Bootleg a) An illicit sound recording of an artist, generally made during a public concert. Under British law, this is not actually illegal if the recording is for private purposes, but it is certainly illegal to offer such a recording for sale.
b) An illegal copy of a sound recording made by a record company but not released officially, then raided from the company's vaults to be copied.

CD or Compact Digital Disc A form of mass-produced digital disc with a diameter of 12 cm, reproduced by laser-beam. The standard form for sound recording was invented by a consortium of Philips and Sony and introduced in 1982. Such discs do not necessarily contain sound; CD-ROMs, for example, contain text which can be accessed by computers.

Cylinder record An early form of record in the shape of a hollow cylinder, with the sound recorded in a spiral groove round the curved outer surface. For many years this was considered superior, because the groove speed remained constant as the record turned, unlike the disc.

Decibel or dB Literally, one tenth of a bel, named after Alexander Graham Bell. Decibels are used for comparing two physical units. They are used in sound recording for both acoustic and electrical work, because they are convenient for comparing two things, (they are not *absolute* units). If two sound powers A and B are being compared, the formula dB = 10 log$_{10}$ (A/B) gives the number of decibels between the two sound powers. Usually, however, we are comparing sound pressures or electrical voltages. For these, the formula is dB = 20 log$_{10}$ (A/B).

Diamond disc Trade-name for a type of disc record marketed by Edison's National Phonograph Company in America between 1913 and 1929. It was the first record designed to be played with a diamond stylus. (Previously, steel or sapphire had been used). The British branch of the Pathé company also made something called a Diamond Disc during the First World War, but this had a different type of groove.

Digital recording Form of recording in which the subject-matter is represented as a stream of numbers (as opposed to Analog Recording). The quality of such a recording is not limited by physical factors, but by how accurately the subject-matter is turned into numbers and back again.

Disc record Form of record in

which the recording comprises a spiral upon a flat surface. The flat surface is therefore usually disc-shaped, although other shapes are sometimes found. If the rotational speed is constant, the actual speed of the spiral under the recording or reproducing heads varies with the radius, which can give rise to some engineering difficulties. In Compact Digital Discs (q v) the rotational speed is varied to compensate for this effect.

Dolby The name of the engineer who invented 'Dolby Noise Reduction', of which there are currently five versions. The aim is to reduce the background noise of a recording without affecting the wanted signal. All Dolby's systems involve boosting quieter parts of the wanted signal before recording it, and applying the opposite treatment during playback, so the signal can override the background noise. The difficulty is to achieve this without the background noise apparently going up and down in a distracting way. The five systems deal with different types of noise and by differing amounts.

Dubbing a) Short for 'Doubling', i.e. copying, any sound recording.
b) Process for adding, or altering, sound for a moving picture, for example from components such as music, speech, and effects.
c) Process for changing the words of the soundtrack of a moving picture from one language to another, and adjusting the translation so the new recording fits the lip-movements of the original actor.

Dynamic range The range (measured in decibels) between the loudest and the quietest parts of a sound performance. When applied to recordings, it is not quite the same as 'signal-to-noise ratio', because the medium may overload gently and the subjective effect of increasing distortion may differ from defined engineering limits; the human ear can also perceive some kinds of sound in the presence of background noise which measures considerably stronger.

Electrical recording Has several possible meanings, but nowadays is taken to mean a sound recording made with the aid of electronic amplification.

Equalization a) An engineering expression used to describe predetermined objective alterations in the frequency balance in the recording process to drown background noise, and the compensating alterations to regain the original balance upon playback.
b) Term applied during the mixing of signals from microphones to alter the frequency balance of sounds for subjective reasons.

Error correction, error detection Terms applied to the process of converting digital signals or recordings back into the original subject matter. 'Error Detection' analyses the numbers in the stream of digits, and detects if an error has taken place. If it has, the equipment may switch to a method of guessing what the faulty subject-matter was, or it may simply alert the operator by warning him something has gone wrong. 'Error Correction' uses additional numbers alongside those of the subject-matter, to rectify errors objectively using an error-correcting code.

Filter In sound engineering, a piece of equipment for removing one or more bands of frequencies. A 'low-pass filter', for example, allows low frequency signals through, but cuts off high frequencies. Such filters may be used for removing high-frequency background noise when a sound recording contains wanted sounds of only low frequencies.

Gramophone Originally the word coined by Berliner for the machine he invented for reproducing lateral-cut analog disc records. Used subsequently as a tradename by various companies officially marketing his machines and later versions. In 1909, a British court ruled that the word had come into such common use it could no longer be a registered tradename, and in Britain it was then used for any analog disc re-

cord player. Not so in America, where the equivalent word was 'phonograph'.

Graphophone Originally the word coined by Bell and Tainter to describe their cylinder machine, to distinguish it from Edison's phonograph. Such machines were first marketed by the Columbia Graphophone Company, and the word is now used to describe any phonograph for playing wax-coated cardboard cylinders six inches long and one-and-three-eighths inches in diameter. The Columbia Graphophone Company kept the word in its official title long after it ceased marketing graphophones.

Groove The means by which sound waves may be recorded and played back by a mechanical pickup (see 'stylus', 'hill-and-dale', and 'lateral'.) Grooves are generally 'cut' out of the recording medium by a cutting-tool, although Berliner used photo-engraving and acid-etching techniques as well. Grooves may have cross-sections of various shapes and sizes, with corresponding different styli to play them.

Headphone Device worn over the head (or inserted into the ear-canal), for converting alternating electrical signals into corresponding sound waves to be heard by the nearby ear.

Hertz, or Hz Hertz was a German physicist whose name was later adopted for expressing the frequency of a wave. One Hertz equals one cycle per second, and 14kHz means 14,000 cycles per second.

Hill-and-dale recording A recording in which the signal is incorporated in a groove of varying depth, so the stylus vibrates up and down as it traces the recording.

Horn In acoustics, a device for matching sounds of low intensity and high dispersion to sounds of high intensity and low dispersion. It is very difficult to make mechanical devices which can vibrate as frequently as sound waves. Such mechanisms have to be physically small, and thus cannot receive or transmit sound energy over a large area. A horn serves to convert sound from one cross-sectional area to another without much loss of energy. Horns of conical shape used to be used for collecting sound from a large area and concentrating it upon an acoustic recording cutter. Various shapes were tried for the reverse process, to match a vibrating mechanism to a large mass of air for general listening, but in the 1920s it was shown that the most efficient shape was 'exponential'. Exponential horns are still used for cinema and public-address loudspeakers because of their very efficient use of energy.

Laser An acronym which stands for 'Light Amplification by Stimulated Emission of Radiation'. A laser gives a coherent beam of light, that is, one in which photons are emitted in synchronous packets. The result is that the light can be directed in a very tight, non-diverging, beam. In the reproduction of sound recordings, it can then be reflected or transmitted by a medium with very closely packed detail, and converted into an electrical signal ready for amplification.

Lateral cut Means of impressing mono sound-waves into a groove, causing it to divert from side to side. A stylus playing the groove therefore vibrates to and fro in the same plane as the medium.

Limiter In audio electronics, a device designed to prevent sound signals from exceeding a fixed limit, while not introducing distortions to the shape of the waveform.

LP or Long-playing record There have been many attempts to make long-playing records, but unless the context means otherwise, the term is nowadays taken to mean an analog disc record with a rotational speed of 33 1/3 revolutions per minute, and a fine groove (or 'microgroove') with a bottom radius less than one thousandth of an inch.

(Invented by Dr Peter Goldmark of the US Columbia record company in 1948.)

Loudspeaker Device for converting alternating electrical signals into corresponding sound waves in air and dispersing them over a suitable listening-area.

Magnetic recording A way of recording by means of an electromagnet in close proximity to a moving medium comprising small permanent-magnet zones (e.g. tape). The advantages are that the medium may be erased and reused by means of an 'erase head', it is possible to squeeze sound and video recordings into small space (with modern magnetic tapes), and that analog magnetic tapes of sound may be cut and spliced without disturbance to the signal.

Matrix In sound recording, a generic term for a family of metal positive and negative versions of a disc record, used in the manufacturing process.

Microphone Device for converting acoustic energy into corresponding alternating electrical energy.

Mono or monaural recording Sound recording comprising one 'channel'. Although such a recording may have been made with several microphones, and may be reproduced through several loudspeakers, no information is lost by reproducing it through just one loudspeaker.

Multi-tracking Way of building up a multi-layered musical or dramatic performance with several sound tracks recorded at different times.

Noise a) In acoustics, a sound without fixed pitch (as opposed to a 'musical note' or a 'tone').
b) In sound recording, unwanted audible material which becomes added to the 'signal'.

Phonograph Word coined by Edison to describe his cylinder record-

ing and reproducing machines. In Britain it has always meant a cylinder machine, but in America the term is applied to any record-player.

Photo-electric cell Device for converting fluctuating light into corresponding electrical signals.

Pirate recording An illicit copy of a sound recording. They are illicit rather than illegal, because many so-called 'pirate' records have been made quite legally in their countries of origin, e.g. Denmark, Indonesia and Taiwan. (*See also* 'Bootleg').

Post-production Originally an expression of the film-industry, meaning the work which remains to be done after the performers have been captured on film. (Eg editing, special effects, sound-mixing). Now the term is used for the analogous procedures in video, sound recording, and even radio.

Pressing A disc record which has been 'stamped' or 'pressed' from a 'matrix', as opposed to an 'acetate' (q v).

Quadraphonic recording Recording intended to be played back upon four loudspeakers all in the horizontal plane.

Shellac A clear resinous organic lacquer originally used as a varnish. It was employed in the manufacture of buttons by the American Durinoid Company, which made some successful experimental pressings for Berliner in 1896. From then on, the sound recording industry adopted the word to describe the mixture of materials used for the majority of sound records for the next sixty years, although shellac was only one component.

Signal Term applied to the wanted parts of a waveform; in sound recording, normally speech or music (as opposed to 'noise', q v).

Sound-box A device dating back to acoustic-recording days for converting sound waves directly into vibrations of a groove cutter, or (reversing the procedure upon playback) the vibrations of a stylus directly into sound waves.

Stereo or stereophonic recording Recording using two channels to give a spatial effect upon reproduction. Originally used both for reproduction on a pair of loudspeakers and on headphones, but now the term is used for the former only.

Stylus A device for interfacing with a groove (q v). A 'Recording' or 'Cutting' stylus is responsible for creating a groove. A 'Reproducing' stylus reproduces sound from a record by being vibrated mechanically. A relatively modern term; previous words for a reproducing stylus include 'needle' (for lateral-cut records) and 'ball' (for hill-and-dale records).

Tape recording Recording made upon a long strip, coiled up on a reel, or into a 'pancake' on a core without supporting flanges. Strictly speaking the phrase should include media such as photographic films, but it is now almost synonymous with magnetic tape recording.

Track-bouncing When sound recording takes place upon a system with several separate soundtracks, the engineers may run out of tracks before the job has finished. The tracks which have been completed may then be 'premixed' onto an intermediate track, so the equipment for the first tracks is released. When this happens on a multi-track machine, sound can be played from several tracks and mixed down to one or two others on the same physical reel; this is called 'track-bouncing'.

Triangle centre Seven-inch 45 rpm pressing made by the British Decca factory in the years 1952 to 1956 with an optional centre in the shape of a triangle.

Two-minute cylinder Cylinder record two-and-a-quarter inches in diameter, four inches long, with a groove pitch of 100 turns to the inch, rotating at about 160 revolutions per minute.

Ultrasonic Higher than the highest-pitched sound which can be heard. Usually *human* hearing is implied, when it means above about 18,000 Hertz.

Valve Device for controlling the flow of something. In the Auxetophone, the device for imparting sound to a flow of compressed air. In electronics, a 'thermionic valve' can be used for amplifying electrical signals by controlling the flow of electrons in a vacuum. (The American word for the latter is 'tube').

Vinyl Short for Polyvinyl Chloride, the plastics material from which most LPs are made.

Wow In sound recording, slow speed variation.

Suggestions for further reading

There are remarkably few books about sound recordings which can be recommended without reservation, and most of those are reference books such as catalogues and discographies, which cannot really be called 'reading matter'. But there are many periodicals. Most record review magazines pay only notional attention to the history of the media, although some (mostly journals of specialist societies) fare rather better. To compensate for the lack of a suitable book, there are a number of very small journals which specialize in publishing newly discovered information about the sound recording industry. Most concentrate upon relatively narrow geographical areas, or different sections of the recorded repertoire. From Britain, I can however recommend *Historic Record* magazine, which seems to have no restrictions in the subject-matter of the recordings it considers.

CHEW, V. K,
Talking Machines
(2nd edition, London, 1981; Her Majesty's Stationery Office).
This Science Museum booklet covers the years up to and including 1914.

GELATT, ROLAND
The Fabulous Phonograph, 1877-1977
(2nd revised edition, Cassell, London, 1977).
The definitive history of the commercial sound-recording industry.

BERGONZI, BENET
Old Gramophones
(Shire Publications Ltd., Princes Risborough, Buckinghamshire, 1991).
Covers the reproduction of sound recordings by acoustic (non-electric) means.

Illustration credits

Pictures are from the British Library National Sound Archive except: Fig. 1 (Science Museum); fig. 3 (Chew *Talking Machines*, 1981); fig. 8 (Read & Welch *From Tin Foil to Stereo*, 1976); fig 8a (EMI Music Archives); fig. 9 (Ann Ronan Picture Library); fig. 10 (Batten *Joe Batten's Book*, 1956); fig. 14 (Gelatt *The Fabulous Phonograph* 1st ed, 1954); figs 15, 15a (British Film Institute); fig.20 (Jack Law); fig. 21 (Marconi); fig 22 (AEG); fig. 24 (Ampex); fig 37 (Chew); fig. 42 (Bernard Roughton); fig. 43 (New York Public Library); figs. 45, 47, 52 (Chew); fig. 57 (British Film Institute).